DREAM ISLAND

A record of the simple life

R. M. Lockley

LITTLE TOLLER BOOKS

This paperback edition published in 2016 by
Little Toller Books
Lower Dairy, Toller Fratrum, Dorset

First published separately as:

Dream Island in 1930
Island Days in 1934

ISBN 978-1-908213-32-7

Introduction © Amy Liptrot 2016
Photographs © The Estate of R.M. Lockley 2016

Typeset in Monotype Sabon by Little Toller Books
Printed in Cornwall by TJ International

All papers used by Little Toller Books
are natural, recyclable products made from
wood grown in sustainable, well-managed forests

A CIP catalogue record for this book is available
from the British Library

1 3 5 7 9 8 6 4 2

CONTENTS

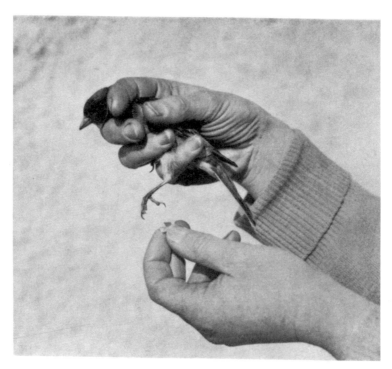

Ringing a chaffinch

INTRODUCTION

Amy Liptrot

M Y RESEARCH into R.M. Lockley and the Welsh island of Skokholm involved a phone call to Gough Island in the South Atlantic, near Tristan da Cunha, one of the world's remotest islands. Over a satellite link shared with a ship and two Antarctic bases, I spoke to Chris, a former colleague from my time working for the RSPB in the Orkney islands where I grew up. Chris was working on a project that required him to camp on tiny, uninhabited Orkney islands for days at a time, catching seabirds and fitting them with tracking devices. Before all this, before Gough Island and Orkney, he had been the warden on Skokholm and Skomer, working for the wildlife trust that now owns the islands. Chris, like me, is both an island and a wildlife lover, and we have made our lives and work in the fields. 'The types of wildlife you get in these places is unique, and there's a different pace of life,' Chris says. In this way, we are the inheritors of R.M. Lockley's legacy.

Dream Island (1930) and his sequel *Island Days* (1934), combined here as a single book, is the account of how Cardiff-born Ronald Lockley moved onto the tiny island of Skokholm, four miles off the tip of Pembrokeshire, where he lived with his wife Doris and daughter Ann for twelve years. Just one mile long, the island had been uninhabited, apart from lighthouse-keepers, since at least the beginning of the twentieth century.

Living as the only inhabitant on your own island is a fantasy for many. It had been a dream of Lockley since boyhood, inspired by Robinson Crusoe and Henry David Thoreau. But, unlike most, he went ahead and did it. Bringing back (human) life back to an abandoned island is hugely romantic. But as well as romance and idealism, Lockley's account reveals the practical challenges and how adventure soon becomes an endeavour.

His restrained, matter-of-fact style is of his time and echoes the books he loved to read as a boy. There are many more technical descriptions of sailing – the state of the boat and the sea, tide and wind – than of his feelings, conversations or philosophy. I admire this practical focus. Lockley wears his considerable accomplishments lightly and is understated about his achievements. In his early twenties, he visits Skokholm and decides 'here at last was my dream island!'. He convinces local fishermen to take him over to the island, speaks to the farmer who rented the island and negotiates the rental of the land for himself – and passes these things off quickly and lightly.

At first, Lockley plans to live on the island alone, but then Doris appears. He charmingly, and briefly, describes their courtship: 'Even now I sometimes wonder if it was because I had an island to offer that she – well, it will suffice to say that very suddenly my lofty plan to be another Crusoe (with a Thoreauvian austereness of life) was completely annihilated. Henceforth I renounced celibacy.'

He travels to Skokholm first to get it ready for Doris to move over. Huge effort is required – he employs local help and takes over the things they need to start a life and begin building. This is a real life adventure including, notably, a shipwreck. The tale of salvaging the contents and material of the wrecked ship the *Alice Williams*, in which they adopt the language of seafarers or pirates ('Ye'd best make the most of her, sir' said John. ''Tis plunder then, John,' I said), is one that will inspire and enthuse readers as much as it did the local men who came out to Skokholm to assist the operation. Timber from the schooner was used in rebuilding the old house and its cargo of coal kept the Lockleys warm for years.

I am also charmed by the bold Doris, respectfully and lightly written by her husband. They are an adventurous and capable couple who choose to honeymoon on Grassholm – an island even smaller and more remote than Skokholm. A few years later, they are joined by their daughter Ann (born on the mainland, brought over to Skokholm at three weeks old).

This island reinhabiting – and, just as importantly, Lockley's writing about it – was an inspiration and model for ideals of island life and self-sufficiency that were to become popular in the second half of the twentieth century. These ideas influenced people like my parents, who bought a farm in the Orkney islands in the 1970s, where I was born. I realise that part of what attracts me to the Lockleys is that they remind me a little of my own family: brave parents and an idyllic but also elemental childhood – playing with lambs, battling with gales.

Additionally, Lockley's ornithological work was an early pioneer of the work now done by contemporary enthusiasts. In 1933, he established the first bird observatory in the UK on Skokholm. He carried out methodical studies of Skokholm's birds, observing their behaviour over years, notably, as described in this book, of the many thousands of manx shearwaters and puffins that breed there. And there is poetry in his science in, for example, how he describes 'the most unearthly coughings and cooings' of the shearwaters and how 'the birds do not like the moon'. In a way, the whole island was his laboratory, and he performed experiments: rabbit-breeding, crop-growing, encouraging bird-nesting, and what we now know as 'habitat management'. This built up into a detailed study of a 'local patch', with decades worth of studies and statistics. Now there are huge ornithological and environmental organisations, RSPB and others, and national networks, encouraging public concern and government policy on conservation – and employment opportunities for people like Chris and me.

Skokholm, and its larger neighbour Skomer, is now a Site of Special Scientific Interest, owned and managed by the The Wildlife Trust of West and South Wales. The public can take a boat over and stay. During Chris's time as warden, the buildings on Skokholm were renovated to turn them back into a bird observatory, with daily rounds, checks for migrants, ringer training and other activities. A warden lives there for nine months of the year. The character of the island is still influenced by Lockley's spirit, Chris says, with visitors coming, inspired by his ideal of island life. Each evening, the current islanders meet for the daily bird log, a long-running tradition.

The concept of 'following your dream' seems like a very modern concoction, but here we have an example of it in the first half of the twentieth century, until it was ended by the outbreak of the Second World War, when the Lockleys were served an evacuation notice. The reader supports Lockley's aims – so clearly defined and hard-won. And, for a few brief years between the wars, his dream blossomed:

> In walking every day around the island upon this work I am able to satisfy my desire to know how my little kingdom progresses, what new arrivals are here, what birds gone: whether the tadpoles are hatched under the starwort in the main pond, whether the lesser black-backs have yet occupied the bog, whether the ravens have brought their young off, whether any black redstarts have come, whether the vernal squills, the campion or the cowslips are flowering, and a hundred other events of early spring.

Amy Liptrot
Orkney, 2016

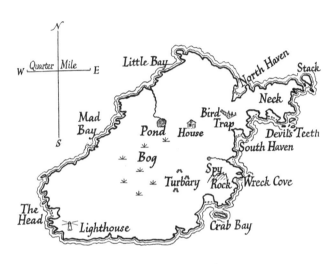

N
W —— E
Quarter Mile
S

Little Bay

North Haven

Stack

Neck

Mad
Bay

Bird
Trap

Devil's Teeth

Pond

House

Bog

South Haven

Spy
Rock

Wreck Cove

Turbary

The
Head

Lighthouse

Crab Bay

The Island

ONE

Daydreams

To dwell alone with birds and flowers in some remote place where they were plentiful and undisturbed was an ambition early cherished in schooldays, as soon as I began to look at, and watch, and so finally to love nature.

This desire became my daily dream as I grew up. In turn I envied the Swiss Family Robinson, the Coral Islanders and Robinson Crusoe. I wished intensely to become a Crusoe. My daydreams led me on wondrous expeditions alone in an open boat, and landed me on isolated bird islands, where I dwelt my hermit life in complete happiness. I built my little hut, kept my goats and my garden, and spent my days in watching and taming birds.

As I learned more about birds and read more books, my dreams even definitely placed me in well-known bird haunts. In turn I enjoyed many islands in the Hebrides, my favourite being the isolated Isle of North

Ronay. I learned, from the map, the names of every small habitable island from the Butt of Lewis to Barra Head and southwards to the Mull of Kintyre. I did not forget the Orkneys and Shetlands, and farther afield the Faroes, Iceland, Jan Mayen, even Spitsbergen, Bear Island, and at the other extreme Tristan da Cunha, Macquarie, the Salvages, Azores, and others.

I loved the more remote islands, but if, at any time, I had been offered one of those nearer home, such as Ramsey or Skomer, I should have been quite wild with delight, and I should not have said anything but a most happy acceptance to an offer of Steepholm, the little islet in the Bristol Channel in sight of my parental home.

These were pleasant if vain dreams, giving me much harmless amusement. I at least learned much about the distribution of birds, and carefully drew up on paper a list of birds which I would see on each of my island refuges.

I shall not mention here details of some of the very wild and unscrupulous plans which I made with a view to achieving the life of a recluse on an island, without carrying them out however.

As I grew up, my choice of authors widened. I read Thoreau very thoroughly, and was so impressed that my thoughts and some actions were for some years quite influenced by his example. I resolved to imitate his austere mode of living when I at last came to dwell on my dream island.

With these dreams and thoughts I left school and rented a small farm on the outskirts of the town where my home had been. The farm was in a pleasant green valley, which attracted many birds, and in consequence I was for several years fairly happy in such an environment, having plenty of work to do. Moreover, my island actually materialised to some extent in the work I set myself to by digging a pond in one field and raising a tiny island in the centre around a venerable oak growing there. Morning and evening in summer before and after the day's work would see me with wheelbarrow, shovel and pick carrying on the great excavation which was to make an island and a pond – sanctuary, I hoped, for pairs of sedge and reed warblers, moorhens, coots and wild ducks. The island I would plant, when finished, with bushes and trees, would provide welcome cover for innumerable birds of every species.

However, it was undoubtedly a big task I had set myself, and would require years of labour. In the meantime my good neighbour and friend, whom I shall call 'Admiral,' came with me once a year, at midsummer, to explore the coast of Wales.

We wandered together in Pembrokeshire, following the coast and visiting the islands one by one each year. Admiral looked at the islands with the eye of a painter, thinking of his brush and palette; I watched the birds, and in this way appeased a little my hunger for islands. Ramsey and Skomer were visited in turn, and the residents there in turn were duly envied by me.

The wonderful bird life on Skomer amazed and charmed us. We had, too, arrived in early June, when the birds and flowers were at their best. The cliffs swarmed with sea birds. The island was carpeted with acres of bluebells, campion, thrift and primroses. It was from the fishermen who ferried us over from Marloes, the nearest mainland haven, that we learned about Skokholm, the lonely uninhabited island which we could see out in the Atlantic south of Skomer. They told us that the same birds and flowers were found as on Skomer, that the farm and the house on the island were in ruins, had been unoccupied for nearly twenty years and that, beyond casual fishermen, and the lighthousemen, nobody cared to visit the place. Apparently it was too lonely and inaccessible; the landing place was very bad; there was no safe harbour; tides swept strongly on all sides, and to get there at all occupied an hour steady sailing, or two or three hours of rowing. In bad weather it was impossible to get near the island.

All this attracted me immensely. I was at once impatient to explore Skokholm. We had, however, already spent two days extra in visiting Skomer, and a return to work was imperative. A south wind blew freshly up through Jack Sound, and we found that while this wind kept up no fisherman was willing to take us down the Sound and out to distant Skokholm.

Through the glasses this lonely island looked most attractive. The ruins of the farm buildings showed clearly in the sunshine, as well as the stone hedges of the old fields. There were wide stretches of pink where thrift flowered, and misty areas of blue where no doubt bluebells spread over the meadows. At the farthest and highest point was the white tower of the lighthouse, facing the open Atlantic, which stretches, without land between, to America. The cliffs were a bright red in the sunshine, and a garland of surf beat and danced beneath them.

We left Marloes vowing to return next year and make a prolonged visit to the lonely isle.

TWO

The Dream Island

M Y DREAMS NOW centred largely on the summer holiday Admiral and I were to enjoy on the faraway and deserted isle. The days seemed to drag by, but at last June again arrived and we set off.

There was a fresh wind blowing when we arrived at Marloes. The fisherman who agreed to take us to Skokholm shook his head over our prospects.

''Twill be rough tomorrow I'm thinkin', the way the wind is now. We can take you to Skomer if you like.'

It proved as he said, a southwesterly wind roughening the open sea where lay the inaccessible island. We spent the day partly in talking to the farmer who rented Skokholm, learning much of its history from him. Although he still rented the island from the lord of the manor, he had long ago given up visiting it. Some twenty years ago he had spent the 'happiest days of his life' living on the island with his wife, when he had undertaken a certain amount of farming with cattle and sheep. Actually, the farm buildings had been in ruins when he had taken the tenancy over, and the farm had not been in proper repair since some time late in the last century. He gave us permission to enjoy ourselves as long as we pleased on Skokholm.

On the third day there was sunshine and no wind. John the fisherman and his mate walked down from Marloes with us to the haven, where the few fishermen of the village keep their boats for shell fishing. Martynshaven that day was bright with bluebells and foxgloves, and the long walk of two miles from the village along the lane to the beach was made pleasant by the corn bunting singing 'a-little-bit-of-bread' to us from the furze-grown hedges, and by lizards basking or darting about in the sunshine.

John's boat, the *Foxtrot*, was launched over the pebbles of the little beach, and in a few minutes we were being rowed out towards ill-famed Jack Sound, dreaded by mariners. We carried a supply of food, our cameras and field glasses.

This was our first acquaintance with Jack Sound, its rocks, shoals and striving tide races. The fishermen rowed the boat into a favourable position: then we felt the current sweep the *Foxtrot* along with great force and carry us willy-nilly down into the open sea. Although there was no wind, the water was white at the outfall of the tide, and the boat danced and bumped unmercifully until we got clear of the strongest current.

'Now you know how 'tis she's named the *Foxtrot*,' John's mate, a voluble fellow, informed us when we were one-stepping in mid-current.

An hour-long pull followed, and another bump through the tide race near the island had to be faced ere we reached the calm water under the island's cliffs.

All the time we had seen birds flying above or resting on the sea in the Broad Sound between Skomer and Skokholm, and now, as we drew in to the latter island, the calm water was strewn with companies of puffins, razorbills, guillemots, gulls, cormorants and other sea fowl – a wonderful sight for a bird-lover. The puffins amused us by their comical expressions. They allowed the boat to come quite close before giving us a last comical look of injured amazement (as it seemed to me). Then they dived suddenly and steeply down into the clear water. We could see them plainly, swimming under the water with short, decisive movements of their half-spread wings. The groups of razorbills, black and white in smart uniforms, gave us a general howl or growl, expressive of alarm and probably annoyance, before flying or diving out of our way. The gulls wheeled far above, protesting with great clamour.

The landing place is in a southern-facing opening in the low cliffs. Here convenient steps run down to meet all states of tide. The fishermen left us at the steps, promising to fetch us in two days' time. They rowed out of the haven to attend to their lobster pots set along the rocky shore.

Shouldering our haversacks, we walked up the steep path to the fields above. We had stepped into a vivid natural flower garden. The sloping banks, the cliff, the very rock, were clothed in a lovely fabric of white sea campion, pink thrift, bluebells, white scurvy grass, late primroses, blue vernal squill, cowslips, foxgloves, yellow lady's fingers, samphire and red sea tree mallows. The whole creek, this south haven of Skokholm, glowed with the flowers, which were wide open to the midday sun.

A path wound through bracken uphill, presently opening out upon a green meadow where stout colonies of bluebells flourished at intervals over the open grassland. The old house and buildings stood snugly sheltered from the southerly wind under a rocky eminence at the highest point of this meadow.

Although birds were running, calling and flying everywhere about us, and I was distracted by their numbers and eager to watch them, the first thing we curious human beings did was to examine the ruined buildings. There was a great fascination in exploring this ancient, storm-beaten dwelling. What sort of home had the islanders made for themselves in the past?

We dropped our packs in the sunshine outside and, not without some excitement on my part, began our exploration. With difficulty we pushed open the rotten and hingeless door of this cottage dwelling. We found ourselves in a roofless porch. Next came an anteroom with three doors leading to three rooms. The doors were rotting to dust, and we had to lift them bodily out of our way. On the right of the anteroom was a small room barely seven feet square, containing an open fireplace and a small ingle built into the wall – evidently the kitchen. There was no roof to this room, but it was occupied by a pair of blackbirds, which had four eggs in their nest on a shelf above the ingle seat. On the left of the anteroom was another room of exactly the same small size, roofless, and floored with large slabs of red island stone. We guessed this had once been the pantry or store, for it had a tiny north-facing window. The middle door of the anteroom opened into the main room of the old dwelling, and here we were greeted by a fine state of affairs.

This living room was floored with decaying boards, and raftered with ancient oak beams, with a sleeping loft above. The blue sky showed through many rude holes in the floor of the loft. One large window had a few good panes left, the rest was boarded over and stuffed with rags.

The best part of this room was occupied by an enormous four-poster bed, built crudely out of driftwood and on the cross boards, which served as a mattress support, were a couple of sacks stuffed with hay and much flattened by pressure. A ruinous old greatcoat served as a quilt. There were, besides, a rough driftwood table, two benches and a genuine old bed cupboard. On the hearth beside the ruined oven and grate were a battered kettle with partly amputated spout and handle, an old brown earthenware teapot in like case and a lately used farm-size frying pan with fat freshly congealed in it. A few broken pieces of crockery, plates and cups to the number of half a score occupied the table in company with some battered forks and spoons, breadcrumbs and crust, and a noble array of shells of razorbills and three kinds of gulls' eggs. From the oaken beams hung a multitude of items: dried rabbit skins, small sacks of full or half-empty, wire snares, dried birds, rags and innumerable sooty cobwebs. A shelf running along one wall was piled with rags, old gin and snares, empty pots and tins, a ruined muzzle-loader, rotten canvas and rope, twine and finally an old family Bible – a 1763 edition. The walls were hung with crumbling plaster and cobwebs.

Into this room we suddenly burst. For a moment we stared in silence. What manner of man lived here? I half expected to see some old miser start up from a dark corner; or perhaps some recluse, some decadent or demoralised follower of Thoreau lived here! These were my first thoughts; but nothing unusual occurred. A mouse ran boldly out upon the table to nibble the crumbs, and the swallows twittered at their nest in the airy loft above. Two doors led from this main room, one to a small roofless room occupied by a pair of wheatears and hanging tufts of flowering pearlwort on the south side, and one to a similar room, roofed partly, and containing an iron bedstead with a broken wire mattress, the whole lashed in place with canvas and rope, on the north side of the dwelling.

Out of doors there were two farm folds surrounded by broken-down walls, and some nine outbuildings; all roofless ruins in possession of the wheatears, stonechats, pipits and hedge sparrows, save the partly tiled barn, the roof of which was still mostly in place.

In complete happiness Admiral and I wandered about the island. Here at last was my dream island! The flowers, stretching for acres over meadow and cliff slope, made Admiral stand and stare often.

He soon had his paints and easel unstrapped. I left him to his painting. Half the island is divided into fields around the farmhouse, the western half, at the extreme of which stands the lighthouse, being quite as wild as nature made it, but heather, bracken and flowers stray equally over both sections of the island. The hedges are of earth supported each side by an outer wall of stones, the latter overgrown by moss and lichen. Rabbits have penetrated these dry walls and made burrows in all the meadows. And, following the rabbits, the birds, too, have made homes in the walls and the meadow warrens.

Mr Puffin, as the fishermen call him, is the star turn of the island birds by day in June. With his smart black wings and tail, his white starched shirt front, his vermilion legs, his enormous red, blue and yellow-striped beak, and his profound air of importance as he looks at you with his clownish brown eye, he compels your attention. From the flat surface of the island many high outcrops of rock rose, and it was on these rocky knolls that Mr Puffin would collect each day after noon. One by one the birds, like so many white-fronted aldermen, would alight and stand close together until the rocks were thickly dotted with puffins. When I approached them they would frequently commence a restless jig with their webbed feet, '*foxtrotting*,' Admiral suggested, and now and then one could imagine that an extra good story was being passed around when one bird after another uttered a profound aldermanic 'Ah – ha – ha.' In his jigs Mr Puffin would sometimes turn completely around, bowing at intervals, as if to his audience, and it might then be seen that his pate was greyish, a touch which completed the aldermanic likeness.

The puffin nests in the rabbit holes. Admiral and I found an egg being zealously incubated at the end of a burrow seven feet long. There were several exits and entrances and inter-subways to other burrows; for it was all part of a warren inhabited by other puffins, by manx shearwaters, and, of course, by the builders and architects in the first place – I mean the rabbits.

The shearwaters were not seen at all during the day, but from 11 p.m. until 3 a.m., in the midnight hours, were very much in evidence. On the first night we were startled and amused by the extraordinary cooing of the shearwaters, which were sitting (on their eggs I presume) in the depths of the rabbit burrows, and an hour or two later, just before midnight, the birds returning from the sea to their sitting mates came flying home screaming, in ever-increasing numbers, until, at last, the whole island resounded with their unearthly cries. I have tried to put the cry to words, but failed.

Kùck-kùck-kùck-öööö

was a typical example, but the birds each have a variation in tone or pitch of note. All the cries are very harsh. Admiral said they were screaming a ferocious 'Appletart! Appletart!' and certainly the cry of birds at some distance was not unlike this word. But the imagination had every opportunity for free rein, so wide was the variation in their weird notes.

The concert was over long before sunrise.

The shearwater, the puffin and the storm petrel were perhaps the most outstanding birds on the island, and were the species that most interested me. Of other birds there was a vast host, particularly of gulls and of oystercatchers. And there were ravens and buzzards, a pair of each.

Manx shearwater at entrance to its nest burrow

Puffins at Crab Bay

I had never been so happy in my life as I was during those three days on this wonderful bird island. I felt that I would never be content until I lived permanently here. Admiral was less sure that he would want to live in quite so isolated a place. He gave me wise counsel from the experience of his years. But the more we discussed my plan, the more I felt it could be carried out, and the more excited I became. Admiral was convinced that I should not be happy until I got my wish. At any rate, in the end, he brought his sympathy and advice to bear on the problem of obtaining the island for ourselves.

We soon found that John and his fishing partner were the mysterious tenants of the old house, and that they slept there on very fine summer nights, mooring their boat off in the calm water of South Haven, and thus saving the time and labour of rowing down to the island from Martynshaven each day. Of course it was a proceeding not without risk, and as soon as the wind increased, or backed to southward, they had to be ready to fly to the mainland.

The men came in at sunset each evening and made a supper of fried bacon and fried gulls' or razorbills' eggs. They then yarned with us for an hour before throwing themselves on the four-poster and sleeping heavily until four or five in the morning. John would snore in tune with the shearwaters that screamed over the housetop, while his mate gradually appropriated the major portion of the bed. We watched this phenomenon with interest in our waking moments, for Admiral and I slept on some hay on the floor by the fire when we were not out-of-doors with the shearwaters at night. At last, when John was in danger of falling out of bed, he would encounter the hard rail of the side, which would wake him forcibly. Thus roused, he would get up, draw his boots on, stir the driftwood fire into life, and cook breakfast. A dozen eggs would be put on to boil in an old saucepan, and those found to be not too far incubated were eaten with bread and butter, and washed down with unlimited tea. The men then went out to fish, and we did not see them again until evening. The egg supply was short one evening when they came in early, so they went off to rob the gulls' nests on the island bog and the razorbills' nests on the rocky slopes of Mad Bay.

Gulls' eggs, we found, were very palatable, even to bird lovers' hungry stomachs. I had no qualms either when I saw how cruelly the black-backed gulls would attack and kill a puffin or a young rabbit, or rob a guillemot of its eggs. There were hundreds of thieving gulls, and we had no trouble in finding their nests in the meadows and in the bog grass. John told us they go on laying throughout the summer if the eggs are taken regularly. He also brought us pollack, crab and lobster, so that we were never short of fish for our supper.

It was a sad day, therefore, when we had to tear ourselves away at last from this island of my dreams.

THREE
An unexpected partner

THERE WERE ANXIOUS MOMENTS when I got home to my farm. I proposed to sell my stock and plant at once, in order to realise some capital for setting up as an islander. Not without considerable difficulty, and more than one perilous interruption of the negotiations, did I at last secure the legal right to dwell in 'the peaceful possession and quiet enjoyment' of Skokholm. Those were the two most anxious months of my life, I believe, when all was in a turmoil of negotiation, of hopes running very high at one moment and correspondingly low at another. Admiral, although he did not propose to come and live with me, being tied by family considerations, was my most faithful and true help throughout all my difficulties.

More complication was to arise, however, when one Doris learned of these plans. Hitherto, Doris had been a friend with whom I exchanged ornithological notes whenever we met, as we often did, being farming neighbours a few fields apart from each other. She would consult me with regard to birds, and I her respecting wild flowers, on which she was undoubtedly an authority.

Now, when I told her all about Dream Island and how I proposed to live alone there, happy with my birds and the flowers, she was sad and full of envy. Even now I sometimes wonder if it was because I had an island to offer that she – well, it will suffice to say that very suddenly my lofty plan to be another Crusoe (with a Thoreauvian austereness of life) was completely annihilated. Henceforth I renounced celibacy. I took an oath on that same sunny day, a certain July 12th, that in one year's time to the very day I would have the island house fit for her to live in. We were to be married, it was agreed, on July 12th a year hence – and we would live happily ever after!

Doris had taken much for granted, had accepted my glowing accounts without reservation. Still, it was only fair that she should see the island, and admire her future home with her own eyes, for at this stage she was already planning house improvements.

Quite a cavalcade of curious relatives accompanied Doris, Admiral and myself down to Marloes. John the fisherman again launched the worthy *Foxtrot*, and ferried six of the bravest over to the island. It was a calm day, and we took two hours to cross with oars only. As we drew near the red cliffs of Dream Island we put out lines to catch our suppers, and were rewarded with both mackerel and pollack.

It was now early August, and the cliff-nesting birds, the guillemots and razorbills, had left, but there were still many puffins, gulls and oystercatchers, and some small land-loving birds. The puffins were busy feeding their nearly fledged young, and all that afternoon could be seen bringing sprats to the nesting holes. With the aid of our glasses we could see that Mr Puffin held three or more sprats in his beak, heads to one side, and tails to the other. Now how does he manage to arrange them so neatly? And how does he catch more than one at a time? We saw a lazy herring gull watching the incoming puffins, now and then swooping down on a bird just about to enter its hole. The puffin would then hastily drop his sprats, which the robber calmly swallowed.

Over the ruined island dwelling five buzzards were soaring. Up and up they soared, wheeling round and round without a flap of their broad wings until they were almost lost in the blue sky. We found later that the buzzards had come for a nefarious purpose: to slaughter the young birds and young rabbits, and to kill any defenceless shearwater which had lost its way or been unable to rise from the bracken overnight.

The visitors were impressed by the lovely colours of the island: the red rocks, lichened in pale green here and there, the purple heather now in flower. Only campion, of the spring flowers, remained in bloom, but there were stretches of goldenrod, ragwort, variegated wild pansies and birdsfoot trefoil.

The gloom and filth of the interior of the old house did not dismay Doris so much as it did her three companions. She boldly cooked the fish in the ancient frying pan and put good heart into all by feeding us well.

There and then she gave me directions for reconstructing the old dwelling to her liking. They were simple enough. I was to remove the partition between living room and anteroom, thus making one large main room; to remove the wall between the little kitchen and the little room on the south side, thus making for her a reasonably large kitchen, where she might carry on in comfort the cooking and baking which would be inseparable from such an isolated home. This, and a roof for her head, was all she asked of me, and she demanded that I should leave as much pioneer work as possible undone that she might eventually share therein.

That evening the living room was looking trimmer than it had been for many years. The cobwebs were swept away and a roaring driftwood fire built up.

Early in the morning we came in from a long overnight inspection of the shearwaters and the storm petrels, and ate our supper-cum-breakfast of fish, toast and tea with hearty appetite.

The storm petrels we found flying like swallows everywhere on the island at night, but especially about the South Haven. Several pairs were nesting in a heap of limestones above the old lime kiln, and we could hear the newly hatched chicks uttering a very plaintive 'Peep-peep'. We uncovered one nest and found both parents tending their solitary, young downy chick. The petrels were nesting, too, in cracks and chinks in the hedge walls, and there was even a nestling in a crack in the outside wall of the dwelling house. These airy little birds, by day restless wanderers on the sea, at night could be seen, though dimly flying with a quick, swallow-like grace, perfectly at home about and over the rocks and walls where they had their young.

A strong wind came with sunrise. The fishermen, who had moored the boat in South Haven overnight, hastened to the house to say that it was time to go. Before we could make ready however, quite a stiff wind was blowing directly into the little haven.

The waves began to rise and roar in and about it.

The fishermen leaped agilely into their boat, which was straining and tossing wildly at its moorings. We were invited to leap after them – from the landing steps. It was an exciting moment, but at last everyone had leaped or tumbled aboard without serious mishap. Fortunately, the three lightkeepers, with whom we had made good friends, had come down from the lighthouse to see us off, and they held the mooring ropes so as to assist us and to pull the boat away from the steps. They waved us goodbye, and watched us sail away swiftly before the rising summer gale.

FOUR

The boat is named

IT WAS NOT WITHOUT fully realising the responsibility of my step, and the possible consequences, that I gave up my farm, selling what I owned – the stock and plant – to the new tenant. I knew that when I had spent my small capital I should be dependent on what I could earn by fishing round, and farming on, the island. The thought nevertheless pleased me. As long as we had the birds, the flowers and the sea, the living, however precarious by accepted standards, would be a constant delight in all others.

Possession of the Island of Skokholm, described as 'comprising 250 acres or thereabouts of rough grazing,' was to be obtained at Michaelmas, and on that date I gave up my farm, taking with me only the few tools and items of furniture, and the books I valued most.

The farmers of Marloes are the most hospitable folk one could wish to meet. While I was on the mainland I never lacked a welcome or a home at any time. This was especially valuable when cold, wet and hungry after a long and stormy crossing from my island, I was assured of a warm fire, good food and a comfortable bed.

It was only a matter of a few months, I was warned, before I would be returning home, glad to be quit of a storm-bound coast, devastated day after day by gales before which nothing taller than a furze bush survived out of doors.

As for living on the Lower Island, as the local people termed Skokholm in contradistinction to Skomer the Upper Island, if the hardy Marloes-born folk could not face it, then surely 'Young Lockley,' arrived out of the hinterland of town life as they supposed, would soon give it up as a bad job.

My first task before finally settling in was to find me a boat. An islander without a boat was unthinkable. To possess a boat that could carry you on expeditions both in storm and calm was to have a valuable possession I soon learned, and in the boat which I subsequently obtained, this, I think, was fairly exemplified.

John the fisherman, whom I now permanently engaged as boatman and general assistant, lent his experience to the selection of a suitable boat. I wanted a boat neither too large to be handled by two men in and about the narrow and dangerous landing place on the island, nor too small to face the vagaries of rough tides and winds on the open sea.

So, together, we examined boats in nearly every haven and port of Pembrokeshire, condemning many. They were all either too large and heavy, or else uselessly small and without engines. In each case, too, the owner seemed to have an extravagant idea of their cash value. An engine was essential in winter to help defeat contrary tides and winds.

Eventually, John approved a rather small boat, about seventeen feet long, with a 2 h.p. auxiliary engine. We were taken for a cruise in it. It was not a new boat, but it was strong and of a good beam and shape. I bought it for £50.

Meanwhile, these days of boat-hunting without result had made me restive to be again on my island. One day I proposed to John that together we should take the fair northeast breeze then blowing and sail down to see how everything was upon that delectable spot. We therefore launched the *Foxtrot*, and went through the Sounds before this opportune wind, under the red lugsail, and at a spirited pace.

The birds had now had the island to themselves for so many months that they seemed very tame when we landed. The summer birds had left, but I was very pleased to see others in their place, including hundreds of thrushes and blackbirds, many starlings, robins and wrens, a few buzzards, falcons and the pair of ravens, whilst about, or on, the pond great flights of lapwing, curlew, mallard and teal. Few flowers were left, but colours still glowed in the October sunlight – red rock, green grass and thrift, russet bracken and heather.

We moored the boat in South Haven and then tried to think out the best means of keeping a boat on the island in bad weather. John told me that the former tenant used to haul his boat up from the tiny beach of red pebbles with a handwinch, winding the boat up on a cable until it rested on the rocky cliff above high-water mark The three lightkeepers came to give their advice, too, and were pleased to learn that someone was coming to live on the island, no doubt thinking of the increased opportunities of posting and receiving mail this would mean for them, among other considerations.

New wire would be wanted for the winch, which was still in working order, having been used fairly frequently by rabbit-catchers and fishermen. I made a list of the many things required for our immediate use.

When we put out of South Haven on our return to the mainland, the sun was setting, and a little owl called us a goodnight from the red cliffs. John bade me take an oar and prepare for a stiff pull along the island shore until we reached the northeast point – at which it would be possible to hoist sail. It was my first acquaintance with a seventeen-foot sea sweep, and I had a grim battle with it.

Soon my wrists and back were aching badly, for the *Foxtrot* was light and resisted the wind with her high freeboard. When at last we could hoist sail, and by a series of tacks with the tide make our way to the mainland,

R.M. Lockley at the tiller of Storm Petrel

I was mightily relieved.

At last my newly acquired boat was delivered at Martynshaven one fine day by its late owner. On the next day, after we had learned how to run the simple little engine, we prepared to make a journey to the island, carrying my furniture and tools, and a rabbit-catcher to work there.

There was a great song in my heart when I loaded my goods and chattels at Martynshaven. First the ponderous *Foxtrot* was filled with chairs and boxes, and then the new boat, my boat, was loaded. Richard, the veteran rabbit-catcher, stepped aboard the *Foxtrot* and we pushed her afloat. Then John and I pushed off the new boat, took the *Foxtrot* in tow with a length of stout rope, and away the infant engine barked, tugging her double load slowly over a flat, calm sea. Though such progress was slow, we had a helping current and got down to the island in but little more than an hour.

We then proceeded to unload and carry the goods up to the old house. Next we tried hauling my boat up over the rocks, using a new wire cable on the winch. There were some nasty gaps in the rocks, but we bridged these with greased sticks, over which the iron-shod keel of the boat slid without difficulty. This, apparently, had been the method here from time immemorial.

When she was at last above the high-water mark of all (and stormy) tides, I admired her in her steep berth. It seemed to me something of an achievement to have hauled a boat up into that cranny in the rocks, and I named her there and then the *Storm Petrel*; like that other seafarer, she flew up to her home in the rocks by night.

Richard was now left in charge of the island, for we had to take back the empty *Foxtrot* to the mainland. Not for the first time had Richard been left thus on the Lower Island, with his supply of food; he was, indeed, one of few men accustomed in past winters to spend weeks alone here; a true philosopher and a steady man at his work, he loved island life.

A fresh northerly breeze had sprung up, and as we slowly pushed along with the tide it increased. When we reached Jack Sound the north wind had already commenced to strive roughly with the north-running tide, and there was a white mass of waves on the notorious Haze or Wooltack Point.

Through this we safely made our way, though soaked and shaken. When we reached Martynshaven the waves were breaking heavily on that north-facing beach, and the problem set us was how to beach two boats safely at the same moment. No good Samaritan was there to help us pull the boats clear of the breakers.

We sprang ashore and each pulled mightily at the bow ropes of both boats, but it was an impossible task for only two. If a big wave threatened, I clung to the Storm Petrel's rope, John to the *Foxtrot*'s. At one moment the boats would lie clear and dry on the pebbles as the breakers sucked backwards, then the waves came curling and breaking in with a rush, slapping the boats and trying to turn them broadside on. We hauled on the painters each time the waves rushed in, but soon the boats were so full of water, and consequently so heavy, that we could pull no more. My own boat was soon more than half full, and the engine quite under water: a tragedy it seemed to me. But we could do nothing now except wait for the tide to ebb, then empty the water out, and haul the boats up above high-water mark.

FIVE

No enemy but winter – and rough weather

O N THE FOLLOWING DAY a southerly gale blew, and this was succeeded day after day by a series of gales, culminating on the seventh day with a hurricane that did much damage to roofs everywhere on the mainland. I wondered how Richard had fared on the lonely island, and whether anything would now be left of the dwelling. At least the roof, I thought, would be entirely gone.

John and I dismantled the *Storm Petrel*'s engine, dried and cleaned it, and at last got it to function again, though it was a long time before it seemed to recover fully from its total immersion.

Nine days after we had left Richard on the island the wind abated enough for us to venture through Jack Sound, and so at long last down to my almost inaccessible home.

Under its snug outcrop of rock the dwelling had weathered the gales well, the rubbish on the roof having been only a little disarranged. But Richard reported that a window had blown in one night and made things so uncomfortable, also that the old house had shaken so much, that he had spent the rest of the night in the open. He asked me if I intended to return at once to the mainland with the dozen score or so of rabbits, some of them already stale, which he had caught for me.

I intended, however, to snatch one night in my new home. Richard looked at the weather and shook his head; however, we hauled the boat up over the crazy slipway, and before dusk I had patched up the roof with enough old tiles and rusty sheet iron I found derelict nearby to make it tolerably rainproof.

A southerly gale came that evening, moaning and whining in the patched-up window crannies. The next morning the sea leaped and thundered in fury about the island. The boat was then safely hauled up to the very wheel of the winch, for the harbour itself was one cauldron of foam and spray. This was the first day of November, and day followed day without a cessation of the gales. John went out to help Richard. It was too rough to attempt house repairs, and so I turned my attention to the ancient garden, a walled-in area in front of the dwelling. Here, where now bracken, briar and nettle flourished, was one day to be sweetly cultivated garden. Day after day I dug and removed the tangle of bracken and nettle roots. The soil was a light-red loam.

I had good company while the gales whitened the sea, for the smaller birds came into the garden for shelter. A few early redwings mixed with the flock, varied each day, of thrushes, blackbirds, chaffinches and meadow pipits. Sometimes a goldfinch would alight on the garden wall, a thick bank of stone and earth; sometimes it was a greenfinch or a flock of linnets or starlings. Often a pair of choughs flew close by, rare, handsome birds that were not at all shy while on the island. At all times there were wrens busily examining the stones of the walls, and the inevitable yet welcome hedge sparrows creeping tamely near my busy spade. Of the several robins on the island, each one in possession of its own territory, from which it drove all others of its kind, there was one so tame that it learned to come into the house for shelter and food day and night.

In the evenings the three of us sat before a roaring fire of driftwood, collected from the creeks and bays of the island. Richard and John would look at the illustrations in my bird and other books. Richard could not read or write, and it was a source of amusement for him to try and guess the names of the more familiar birds. At other times he would sit upright and silent in the armchair I had provided for his old bones, talking a little to himself and zealously keeping the fire ablaze and cheerful by gentle pokings and fuel.

I had constituted myself head cook and bottle-washer, and generally had plenty to do, but in the dancing blue and red flames of the driftwood fire I could build up my castles and dreams of the future. Out-of-doors the wind shrieked, and the sea was all a smother of white horses and wind-driven foam. From the house the view of the mainland, of Jack Sound and of Skomer, is bold and grand, but it was especially fine with the sea leaping up every cliff. Steam and sailing ships constantly passed between Skokholm and the mainland, making for the shelter of Milford Haven, at the entrance to which stands the lighthouse of St Ann's. At night this bright lantern would send its intermittent light through the window upon the wall of the little room, where I slept alone.

To be on the island was a great joy to me, and the difficulties and trials that confronted me at every turn made me all the more eager to attempt to overcome them.

Many of the earlier-caught rabbits were now stale, and had to be thrown away, but at last, on the fifth of November, the wind veered to the northwest and we made haste to leave. With difficulty the boat was lowered over the crazy planks, the rabbits loaded and the engine started. No sooner had we reached the extreme point of the island, the tall Stack rock, and had begun to put across to the mainland when a gale began to spring up and we were driven back again. Our troubles were not over, however, for, in hauling the boat up again, a timber bridging a large hole in the rocks suddenly cracked in two, letting the boat down abruptly upon a sharp rock edge. A nasty hole was torn in her side.

The ever-useful John, however, mended the rent with lead, tacks and tar, and we waited for the next favourable day; but this did not come until two days later, when the weather moderated enough for us to venture again upon the sea passage.

When we had sewn an outfit of sails for the *Storm Petrel* I was more pleased than ever to own and use her, for with her new lug and jib sails she was capable of tackling all but the roughest seas. Now when the engine was swamped by heavy spray and unwilling to function we were not dependent on oars; the sails would carry us where we wished. With both engine and sails she would drive forward at a grand pace. Often there was no need to use the engine, when the gales blew us, under reefed lugsail only, across to the mainland; for it was easier to fly from the island before a southerly wind than to get back again. We seemed to get very few of those desirable northerly and easterly breezes, which, blowing from the land, could not raise an angry sea, and which were so favourable for a swift passage to my island home.

Each crossing was an adventure, and, to me, an achievement; sometimes a calm passage, but more often a rough and a swift one. We fought contrary tides by helping the engine with oars, or contrary winds by beating and tacking, the engine enabling us to sail very close to the wind. Nevertheless, we were often beaten and driven back, forced to land on unsuitable beaches or to fly back whence we came, taken aback by a stormy shift, or increase, of wind. There were many setbacks and disappointments, such as rabbits lost by staleness through inability to market them, and the impossibility of returning to the island for days at a stretch.

Yet every day there was a wonderful song within me. I enjoyed every adventure, admired every mood of sea and sky, and as the days passed began to look forward to spring and the return of the summer birds, and so to summer and the many things that must come to pass then.

I believe I was the happiest mortal in the world.

There were, of course, a hundred and one things to be done, and I chafed at the delay caused by being weatherbound ashore on the mainland. But I soon learned to use every fine day to cross with the rabbits, which were an important source of revenue. So that, when I had learned each intricacy of tide and current from St Ann's Head to Jack Sound, I was more capable of judging whether we could make a favourable passage, and at what time we could return. Always I considered how to overcome the contrary tide in order to get home again on the same day, for I hated being idle on the mainland when there was so much important and interesting work to be done on the island.

The crazy shipway in South Haven was a great source of danger to the boat, and this was one of the first jobs that cried for attention. The present and past method of bridging the gaps in the rocks with greased planks, for the keel to slide over, was a laborious business. Often the rough seas would wash them away either before the boat landed or after it had passed over them. To build a solid slip of concrete was far too expensive a project, and in winter there was a likelihood of the whole being swept out by one of the terrible ground seas that pounded into the haven after each gale. It seemed to me that the best thing to do would be to bridge the gaps with something heavy and permanent, such as a series of iron rungs bolted to the rock, so as to make a sort of ladder up which the boat could slide. John and I talked it over and finally agreed that this was the only thing to be done under the circumstances.

At last, when I had almost decided to send to the nearest foundry, many miles away, for the required angle iron, we noticed two strange-looking objects beneath the boulders in South Haven, and but a few yards from the landing beach. A heavy ground sea had recently displaced some of the great red boulders on the beach and had brought to light two long spars, partly green with weed, partly bare through the chafing of the pebbles. They were of iron, and when we had dragged them from beneath the rocks it was plain that we had discovered the very thing we required. The two spars were of angle iron, and must have been part of some ship's boat or barge, for John now recollected an old tale of a boat driven ashore in a gale in South Haven. These irons were evidently the sole remnant of that boat, the wood having long ago drifted away. The irons were each at least thirty feet long, and put together framed the gunwale line of the boat thus ()

Storm Petrel at her rocky birth

Here was a marvellous piece of good fortune for us. With considerable difficulty we hauled the heavy irons up above high-water mark, and then spent several days in cutting them up into iron rungs of the required sizes to bridge the gaps, straightening the rungs in a fire, and finally bolting them down upon the rocky slipway. We drove holes in the rock with a rock chisel and cemented the bolts into these holes, and thus, in time, achieved a ladder for the boat at almost no expense. The keel could now slide easily over greased, hardwood bars which were then permanently fixed in the angles of the iron rungs.

The sea had given us these irons, as it had given, and daily continued to give to us, enough driftwood to keep us warm with bright fires. Especially when southeasterly winds blew did the sea leave for us in South Haven, Boar's Bay, Peter's Bay, and Crab Bay, those southward-facing openings in the cliffs, a quantity of timber. It is true that nearly all of it was small and fit only for firewood, but occasionally a useful spar or plank drifted in. These I put aside to be used for the house building. Other prizes and surprises the sea gave us also: boxes and bottles filled and empty, bunches of candles, fruit, glass floats, corks and other useful items.

November and December passed, and they were months of storm and wet. But when the slipway was finished I was happier about the *Storm Petrel*. We found we could now launch the boat over the iron ladder in quite rough water with safety, and in this way we were able to get away more often and so save the rabbit crop.

I began to love being out in the boat, sailing upon the current-wracked sea. The cormorants, shags and gulls were pleasant company in all weathers, and sometimes we saw red-throated and great northern divers, and little auks – all wanderers from colder seas. Often, too, we went out in weather not fit for an open boat. Now that I know the sea better, and respect it more, I sometimes think with amazement of the number of times we did so venture; when the sea beat inboard, and of how many times the lee rail was awash as we lay down to a stormy beam wind, under reefed sail.

When on the island I at once turned my attention to repairing the old barn. This building I intended to make habitable enough to live in while we were dismantling and repairing the old house. I did not intend touching the house until the spring, when I hoped for better weather, but meanwhile I tackled the barn, taking up a trowel for the first time in my life. To engage a mason, besides being an expensive business, was almost an impossibility. Almost no one would face the work and life here in the winter, for some reason I could not entirely fathom, though I guessed at it.

John was at hand to advise, in between his usual work of assisting Richard, and by Christmas time I had repaired the roof and walls of the barn. For mortar we dug a fine earthy sandpit under an outcrop of rock in the middle of the island. This earthy sand, mixed with equal parts of lime and of ashes (from the large, ancient midden near the farmhouse door), made a very cheap, strong mortar. With patience and practice I learned to build up the gaps in the walls first, and then, encouraged, went on to repair the roof. New rafters and plates were necessary in one place and here the driftwood timber was employed. I put in for a wall plate a solid oak plank which should last at least a century. Laths were laid across the rafters, and I next gathered the fallen tiles and sorted them to their sizes, the largest at the eaves and smallest at the ridge. Each tile had to have a wooden peg to hang on to the laths by, and a bed of mortar to rest upon above the preceding row. It became a fascinating, if slow, task. But I was pleased because everything except the lime was produced on the island. Even the tiles had been dug from the little quarry on the island many years ago; they were irregular, thick and heavy, but of a pleasant, yellowy grey colour.

SIX
Lower Island Lodge

IT HAD BY THIS TIME become clear to me that I should need some shelter of my own to which I could retire when forced to stay on the mainland during bad weather, instead of, as hitherto, burdening the hospitable farmer with an often unexpected guest. Therefore, the new year found me building a little hut on the bluebell slope above the haven where my boat rested when I was ashore.

Martynshaven is two miles away from the village, and from where I built the hut, overlooking the haven and the wide bay beyond, there was no house or farm visible. I was happy to have the haven to myself, and I knew that a certain lady would be pleased too. Was not the steep slope in front of the hut full of bluebells, foxgloves, lizards and birds in summer? Pairs of stonechats and linnets and whitethroats lived in the furze and bramble thickets. There was, too, a spring of water at the foot of the slope.

While I worked there upon the hut, I was almost as happy as if I had been working at Skokholm. John worked with me, and at intervals we voyaged down to the island to tend Richard and bring back rabbits.

We made this hut into two rooms, first digging into the steep slope for a deep, secure foundation that would hold against all gales. One room was to be the living room, and the other for storing goods. At midday, every day of the week, the post boy brought me great treasure – a letter from the uncrowned queen of the island. When Thoreau was building his hut he read the newspaper his lunch was wrapped in. It was a great pity, thought I, that he had none such as I had to write his news for him.

Sometimes we stayed a few days on the island, carrying on with the work of converting the barn. John now worked all the time with me. He proved to be a clever mason, though he had not done such work before, and I now foresaw we should ourselves be able to do all the repairs on the island.

Early in February the mainland hut was finally lined and completed, and duly named, perhaps a little facetiously in view of its size, 'Lower Island Lodge.' Now I was free to turn my whole attention to the island buildings, but, happy in that, when forced to stay ashore, I had my own roof under which to shelter.

The work on the barn occupied so much of my time that I could ill spare any for the necessary routine of cooking meals and house cleaning; nor could I spare John from his work. But my luck still stood, for I now received a letter from my one-time farm assistant, Henry, a boy of sixteen. He was out of work, and he wrote to ask if I could fulfil a hope I had once given him of employing him on the island. Henry was a nice young lad, much given to reading pirate and adventure stories, and he had, I believe, a very picturesque idea of what life on an island in the High Seas was like; so I gave him the necessary instructions for getting down to Marloes and joining me.

February was a month of fairly quiet weather. The winter gales and rough seas gave way to cold easterly winds, with frost on the mainland but rarely on the island. At the beginning of the month we had had one bad crossing: the last of the gales, taking us suddenly aback as we were entering Jack

Sound en route for the mainland. Before we could run the sail down in order to reef it the violently increasing wind snapped the yard in two, and, a moment later, as the boat bumped over a high wave, the mast was jerked out of its step. Mast, sail and broken yard all went by the board; the mast splitting athwart in two at the same time through being unstepped and the consequent pressure on the clamp. With difficulty we saved the precious sail and mast, hauling it inboard again by the halyards, which were still fastened in the cleats. We then drifted through the Sound before the wind, pulling with the oars until we gained shelter and relief behind the Haze Point.

Spring was coming rapidly to the island. In January frogs had spawned in my two ponds, and now, in February, the shearwaters were returning to the rabbit burrows, for they began their absurd calling and cooing in the middle of the month. The herring gulls sat two by two sedately on the cliffs, evidently paired off and waiting for summer and the nesting time. The great black-backed gulls called amorously and wheeled and circled endlessly above the island. They had never deserted us, even in stormy mid-winter. The 'sea pies,' as John called the oystercatchers, now invaded the meadows in couples, and made day and night merry with their 'ki-ki-ki-kivi-kivi-kivi' ad infinitum. The lapwings behaved in mad and merry fashion as they flew erratically over their breeding ground on the island bog. Larks and pipits sang airily on sunny days, and, in the garden now dug from end to end, blackbirds and hedge sparrows sang tunefully. Primroses and lesser celandines were opening out, and South Haven gave promise of being a carpet of flowers once more.

Lintels had to be put in the walls of the barn to take the four windows and the door. So we pierced the walls, which were two feet thick, very carefully, and inserted heavy lintels cut from driftwood planks. Then windows and door were fitted and built in, making the barn light and warm.

It now remained to build the fireplace and chimney shaft. However, while we were engaged on the foundation of this, a fresh adventure was sprung upon us.

SEVEN

The wreck of the Alice Williams

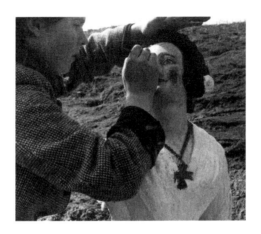

MANY ARE THE TALES of wrecks on this coast. The Lower Island has had its share of them in the past, when ships were made of wood and did not sink easily, but more often drifted ashore on some unfriendly coast. Indeed the men of Marloes complain that they do not have a wreck on the coast now more than once in a decade, because modern-built ships sink on the spot. There is a legend that Skokholm is ringed around with wrecked vessels lying a few fathoms deep, and that is the reason why, so the folk say, there is now a lighthouse on the island.

Howbeit, one morning late in February, I strolled out of doors, early and eager to work, there to find, fast in the rocky cliff below tall Spy Rock, a fine old wooden schooner with all her sails spread to the now gentle southeast breeze! There had been a strong wind all night, accompanied by heavy mist, and now here she was – a wonderful prize.

When you have lived long enough (it need not be very long!) on a sea coast, everything that the sea gives up you grow greedy to take. You even dream of a great ship crushed on the beach, pouring out its lifeblood of innumerable spars and canvas, tools and treasure, which you will be greedy to fight for, steal, and hide from the sight of preventive officers. You think rather less of the possible loss of life than of the spoils of the wreck. In short, a wreck proves to you how avaricious you really are. I believe my first thoughts when I saw the schooner were as discreditable as any confirmed beachcomber's.

Looking directly down upon the schooner from the high cliff above, I was able to admire and to pity her to my heart's content. The tops of her topmasts were on a level with me. Her two large sails, the main and fore, were all set, as were her two topsails, the upper and lower, on the foremast. Her bowsprit, in striking the cliffs, had broken off short, the stump leaning out over the lower cliff in such a way as to form a convenient gangway for agile persons. The jibsails, or headsails, were torn to shreds, which hung in the stay wires of the broken bowsprit. The ship itself was quite fast in a cleft in the cliff. She had evidently blown in at high water, ramming her stern against the sheer cliff on one side, and her bow against the shelving rocks of the other side.

The decks were in confusion when John and I boarded her. Ropes and chains were strewn everywhere, but there was no sign of life aboard, only the gentle swaying of the sail yards and booms in the breeze that could no longer move the fastened ship. The sea washed in and out below decks, filling the cabin, the hold and the fo'c'sle.

A peep into the hold revealed the cargo. Instead of gold and silver ingots, as almost hoped for but not expected in these degenerate days, the hold was full of black diamonds – coal! There must have been two hundred tons of coal on board the good old *Alice Williams*, for that was her name, painted and carved on bow and stern.

When I looked over the bulwarks down into the now almost calm sea I saw much wooden wreckage floating close to the ship's side. The enormous rudder, torn out of its seat, was half afloat and half sunk by the weight of the iron fastenings on it.

Then quite suddenly I saw amid the wreckage a woman's face – a strong, bright face with piercing blue eyes that gazed far-seeing into the blue sky. The woman still wore her hair neatly coiled, with a black ribbon and red roses still twined in it. She also wore a white frock with an old-fashioned tight bodice, and around her neck was a rosary of jet and a black cross that matched her raven hair. She floated serenely on the water, despite the fact that one of her arms was missing.

'Quick, John,' I cried – 'a rope here, boy!'

Again and again we threw a rope with a hook on the end down to the floating lady. She took not the slightest notice of our frantic efforts for her rescue. At last the grapple caught in a coil of her hair and without any ceremony we hauled her up bodily over the ship's rail. It was *Alice Williams* herself, the serene and proud figurehead of the schooner, dressed, as she was first conceived, in the fashion of the 1850s. True to her ship she had stayed to the last, even when struck off by the rocks and when all the others had abandoned it.

We propped her up beside the ship's wheel on the poop, and I then paced the decks wondering what to do with this prize ship. Would she move out of her rocky berth? I could but try.

'Stand by there, John, my lad!' I bellowed, taking the wheel from Alice. 'Cut anchors and hoist the flying jib; we'll away to London Town and sell this good ship for a thousand golden doubloons!'

'Aye aye, sir!' cried John, who in his day had served on more than one schooner and ketch. 'Hey there, bos'n, fetch the crew and step lively to it! Up aloft wi' ye and shake out the foretop skysails!'

The gulls laughed back at us, and the high cliff echoed, but the ship never moved. She was in her last haven. Her wooden sides and keel had settled once and for all in the cradle of red island boulders. The wheel shaft had broken off near the rudder post, and there was a hole in her bows from which coal already leaked.

'Ye'd best make the most of her, sir,' said John. 'In a day of wind she'll be swept to the bottom.' ''Tis plunder then, John,' I said. 'We'll save what we can.'

Below deck, as the tide ebbed, we found the cabin, fo'c'sle, and sail room in great disorder and full of broken panelling, planks and timber. The captain's instruments, the ship's china and kitchenware were washed away already, but I saw my opportunity to lay in a stock of coal to last me for many years. It remained to get together enough hands to work the cargo out of the hold and on to the ledges of the cliff – no easy task, I was to find.

That day John and I lowered the brand-new mainsail and the old red foresail and cut them from the bolt ropes. On the end of the lower topsail yard, which leaned out towards the cliff, we fixed a block, and through it reeved a rope to the ship's winch. John turned the winch while I fastened the sails one at a time on to the rope. Up and up soared the folded mainsail until it touched the block on the end of the yard and, hanging thus over the cliff and the ship, could go no higher. Then I climbed ashore, and as John lowered the rope slowly pulled the great heavy canvas down on to the cliff. In this way the foresail was hoisted ashore, and finally *Alice Williams* herself was tenderly swung up to the yard and down to the cliff. There I leaned her against the rocks in such a position that she could watch all subsequent proceedings on her wrecked ship.

EIGHT

Alice signs her last crew

As henry was expected at Marloes the next day we went ashore to fetch him. I also took the opportunity to ring up the local ship's underwriter in order to put my salvage operations on a legal footing, a necessary proceeding even on a remote island.

From the underwriter I learned that the *Alice Williams* had got out of control in the night, her headsails having been carried away by the gale, and, as she was in danger of drifting on to the rocks in this unmanageable state, anchors were dropped. These, however, dragged, so, after sending up distress flares, the crew of five finally lowered the ship's boat and abandoned the schooner. They were later picked up by a trawler near St Ann's and taken to Milford Haven.

I bought the good ship *Alice Williams* over the phone for the sum of £5, anchors and chains not included.

Henry was mightily excited about the wreck and impatient to see the island. Richard had now finished his catching for the season, so we had brought him ashore, and now took Henry back in his place. There was also a lorry-load of slates, lime and other gear, for the rebuilding of the island dwelling, waiting shipment at Martynshaven. I decided, therefore, to load up the *Foxtrot* and to sail down in her instead of using the *Storm Petrel.*

A stiff southeast wind was blowing when we put out for Jack Sound, and we were deeply loaded with over a ton of material. In addition I had put on board the handwinch I usually kept on the mainland beach for hauling up my boat, as I thought it might be useful to use, in partnership with the schooner's winch, in salvage work. But, in spite of such a steadying load for our sail below Jack Sound, the wind increased to such an extent that we could not beat down to the island, even with a strong tide in our favour. Henry's first crossing was likely to be an exciting one; an introduction to the island for him to remember long afterwards.

Almost before we realised our danger the wind began to strengthen still more. A squall of rain helped this increase, and we began to blow out of the helpful current into slack water under the lee shore of Skomer. It was too late to run back through Jack Sound, for we could not fetch there, and in a very few minutes we expected to be wrecked ourselves on the wind-tossed sea beating on Skomer's rocks. Poor Henry, now alarmed in addition to being very sick, crouched helplessly in the midst of the cargo. John held to the tiller, trying desperately to manoeuvre the *Foxtrot* into Jack Sound, while I pulled an oar to help whenever the lurching boat allowed me to dip one.

One chance seemed to be left to us; to try to run up through the Little Sound between Skomer and Midland against the tide. By so doing there was just a chance of escaping from the southeast gale, saving ourselves and incidentally the boat and cargo. The current in Little Sound is notorious for its strength at any time, and today marked the top of the spring tides.

We entered the narrow neck of this sound at a moment when the ebb current was at its strongest; actually at low water, when the seas roared down southwards to meet the blast of the wind in direct opposition, so raising a tumultous barrier of broken water. Into this white smother the

Foxtrot plunged willy-nilly, driven before the rising gale.

It was now a contest between tide and wind. The current hurried us southwards, the wind blew us northwards; the sea merely tossed us about unmercifully, and dashed water inboard at every motion. John held grimly to the tiller, skilfully keeping the boat head-on to the current and the breaking water. When we reached the strongest part of the tide we also reached the point where the wind was strongest, and that was at the narrowest part of the Little Sound. Nevertheless, the wind was not strong enough to enable us to beat the tide; one neutralised the other, and we were, to all appearances, anchored under full sail in a roaring torrent.

How long could we keep the boat head-on to the rough water? One misguided touch of the tiller might slew the boat round broadside on and then all would be over. Again, it would not be very long before the spray would about fill the boat, and then one big wave would settle the matter by sinking us. Worse still, the current was not due to slack for at least another two hours.

When I saw we were not making headway through, I scrambled forward and again began using an oar to help, and it was the maddest rowing I have ever put hand to. At one moment the oar would be half-buried in a rising wave, at the next waving fruitlessly in the air. Yet the little extra pull, when I was able to make it, gradually helped us against the roaring tide.

I sat with my back against the mast and pulled with all my heart.

A little later, however, the blade of the oar was drawn down very suddenly by a high wave. I strove to slip it out of the water by twisting the oar until the blade was on edge, but was not quick enough. The handle, forced by the pressure on the blade, came up against my chest, my back being already against the mast. Something was bound to give way, and a second later the oar obliged, for it snapped in two at the rowlock. We then began to lose way and drift down the Little Sound again.

John had cried from his boatman's heart a desperate 'Ah!' as he saw his prized eighteen-foot oar snap and go by the board, and he looked at me dubiously as I took up a heavy, fourteen-foot one. However, it was necessary to get out of the smother before we were swamped, and he himself dare not leave the tiller for one second.

I used the utmost caution with this second oar and gradually helped to work the *Foxtrot* out of the seething tide race. Then, just as I had relaxed my efforts, a little exhausted, the oar was again trapped suddenly by a wave, I was pinned against the mast by the handle, and at once snap! went the heavy oar. There was now but one oar left to us, a pretty predicament should we be forced to row, as, indeed, we soon had to.

We were now clear of the worst tide and were safely in the shelter of the Skomer north cliffs, but to get back to the mainland was our next problem. It would mean a stiff row along under the cliffs and across the smooth upper side of Jack Sound to Martynshaven – but with only one oar.

Any port in a storm is a true saying. We could not row with but one oar, so we sailed on into the north haven of Skomer, that calm and spacious harbourage, sailed right on to the landing beach. I then jumped out, ran to the boat belonging to the island resident, and, as there was no one in sight to beg or borrow from, took one of the four oars lying on the beach beside the boat. With this oar to match that last one in the *Foxtrot* we at last succeeded, after two hours of weary pulling, in reaching Martynshaven.

Poor Henry, huddled all the while in the stern, wet, sick and bedraggled, was helped ashore, the cargo unloaded and the boat hauled up. And as if to mock at our plight, the storm passed away shortly afterwards.

The next day was marvellously calm, and I was early astir seeking oars to replace the pair I had broken. I was recommended to a certain master mariner, owner of a coasting ketch, and on visiting him at his home at Sandy Haven was courteously given a spare pair of oars.

Sandy Haven lies within the shelter of St Ann's Head and the calm waters of Milford Haven. There is freedom here from the surge of the Atlantic. Trees fringe the tide line on each side of the inlet, and rarely does the gale shake the tall tops of the beeches which the high land shelters so securely. Captain Cristal's ketch lay moored against the little quay on which his house abutted, the whole forming a charming picture in this winding wooded inlet.

The spirit of adventure seized Captain Cristal when he learned of the wreck of the *Alice Williams*.

'I'll come with you and help save all that coal. It's a windfall. There might be some useful ropes and gear there, too, to suit the old ketch; she needs them sorely. I'll come along with you now.'

And so saying he did come. He packed a kitbag and roused out a second hand, a jobbing labourer, to come with him. At Marloes we picked up John and Henry, and, strange to say, the mason whom hitherto I had been unable to induce to come and repair the island house. The wreck proved a better lure to the mason. But I was glad to have him to help us; and I promised him a boatload of coal for his services. So, at the last moment, there was an assembly of six on the beach at Martynshaven: Captain Cristal and Billy his man; the mason and John; Henry and myself.

Alice Williams had weathered the storm of yesterday easily, for it had come and gone at low water, while the sea had ebbed quite away from her. When all the newcomers had admired the wreck and trod the decks till the novelty of doing so had worn off, we set to work, and carried on merrily for several days. John and the mason wound the winch which hoisted the coal out of the hold by the basket-load. Cristal and Billy loaded the baskets, while I pulled them in to the cliff and piled the coal on the ledges. It was very heavy, hard work On the third day Cristal missed his footing on the deck and fell into the hold. Luckily, the tide had just begun to fill the ship, so that he had nothing more hurtful than a swim in dirty water, but, until he emerged, black and wet, we were mystified by his sudden and complete disappearance. Even this fall did not damp his merry spirits, which were at all times the life of this strangely assorted crew.

Henry, a delighted grin perpetually on his fresh young face, helped, in between his duties as head cook and bottle-washer. When we were thirsty between meals he brought us an enormous kettle (ex *Alice Williams*) of tea. He was detailed to get our supper, which consisted of a saucepan or two full of boiled potatoes, swedes and salt beef ('ship's junk' from the pickle chest of the *Alice Williams*) – a simple enough supper, but one to which our ravenous appetites did full justice.

Henry, as a matter of fact, was living a life highly to his taste. He had stepped from prosaic farm life into High Adventure amid island, sea and wreck. He gazed at first in awe at the stranded schooner, treading the decks circumspectly and looking giddily up at her tall masts.

'Do you think I could climb the rigging?' he asked on the first day, as he watched the experienced John run up to the crow's nest like the proverbial cat, adjust some ropes in the masthead blocks, and presently come sliding down on a hand rope at a reckless pace.

'Up with you, lad. Tumble to it!' I replied, and up he went, very gingerly and not very far the first time.

After supper in the old house the six of us would gather before a roaring fire of new coal from the wreck, and yarns flew around until midnight. Captain Cristal had an inexhaustible supply of personal adventures and anecdotes, while the mason ran him a close second and tried to out-talk him. Cristal led the laughter at the end of each of his yarns and compelled us all to join in, if only because the heartiness of his laugh amused us. Henry gaped through each yarn, and then laughed so immoderately that Cristal would turn to him with an enormous smile and say, 'Good heavens, boy! What's the joke?' and thus set Henry off into hysterics.

When we were all too tired to talk we fell asleep. Henry and I shared my little room; John and Billy slept on some hay on the floor; the mason and Cristal shared the big driftwood four-poster, and all night long grumbled and quarrelled over the division of territory upon it.

Some time before dawn the energetic Cristal would relinquish his share of the bed, to the profound relief of the mason who was now able to snore in peace, and stir up the dying fire. This was the signal for a general uprising. When breakfast, consisting of the inevitable bacon, bread and butter, and tea, was ready, the mason put his boots on and joined us. Thus the day's work began somewhere about sunrise, and went on until sunset.

The sea, at high water, was on a level with the schooner's deck, and it was not possible to work then for an hour or two, so we spent this period in hauling the coal, sails, rope and gear already ashore on to higher ground, using my handwinch, which was mounted on the top of the cliff.

Each tide had its effect on the *Alice Williams*, working and prying loose more and more of her planking. Soon the keel was pressing up through the ship, each day lifting the masts a few inches higher above the sinking deck. At high-water the whole ship rocked gently to and fro, the masts swaying and creaking ominously. The first breeze or ground swell must inevitably bring her total dissolution. Therefore, we toiled each day until we were worn out, trying to save the coal that at each tide leaked by the ton out of the rent in the bows. But after four days' work we had piled up enough coal, I hoped, to last me many years.

We began to strip the decks as soon as the rising tide made work dangerous in the hold. First the cook's galley, a little deck house not more than six feet square, was unshipped and bodily chained for removal. The winch slowly wound this shanty up to the yard arm just like any basket of coal, and we had the unique sight of a cook's galley dangling fifty feet up on the topsail yard. Then the other winch slowly pulled it in to the cliff, while all below hid their heads in anticipation of something giving way.

In this manner, too, the main topmast of the schooner was unshipped and hauled ashore, for I had my eye on this for a flagstaff.

The tiny wheelhouse was deemed too heavy to lift to the yard arm; it was therefore thrown overboard and towed by boat around to South Haven, where it was finally rolled up the broad landing steps to a safe place on the grass. Cristal secured for his ketch some heavy mooring and towing ropes, some gaffs, booms and other useful items.

At the end of six days most of the coal had been washed out of the hold, and the old schooner was tilted at a sharp angle, awaiting her end. The masts were askew and only held in place by the stout rigging. I believe there were tears in Alice's eyes, but to spare her the final agonies I carried her up to the top of Spy Rock beside the island flagpole. Here she might still breast a salty wind and look out over restless seas, with foam and white water below her.

It was now getting too risky to work on board. The neap tides did not entirely leave the schooner by day. Moreover my crew were thoroughly exhausted, ready to give up and depart to civilisation once more. So we put them ashore, with due thanks for their voluntary services.

Two days later there came a half-gale from the southeast and the *Alice Williams* was totally destroyed. The wind and sea piled her fragments high on the island beaches. I was able to select all and more than I wanted of oak beams and other timber for the reconstruction of my future home.

NINE
The Wheelhouse

WITH MARCH, BIRDS FLOCKED in still greater numbers to the island, the early spring arrivals mingling with the winter visitors. In the middle of the month the wheatears arrived, dozens of them flying low about the stone hedge walls, bobbing, curtseying and calling 'Jack, Jack,' to me. The lesser black-backed gulls came quite suddenly to occupy the island bog. They sat together in pairs on the long grass, and resented with loud cries the approach of any human form. The ravens had long built their nest on the cliff in Mad Bay, and now had a ravenous young brood of five to feed. They had built a strong nest of dead heather stems and roots, and had lined it warmly with fibres and rabbits' wool. Late in the month came the chiffchaff, and flights of starlings, rooks and chaffinches – all transitory visitors, hurrying in some northerly direction to their breeding haunts.

Primroses were at their best, growing in the bays and on the slopes of the island cliffs. South Haven was yellow with primroses and lesser celandines. Sea campion and violets were just beginning to flower.

While we were occupied in building the barn my thoughts turned much on the future. This first year I would not have time to be a fisherman; the summer would pass all too quickly in house building. Yet it was all very well to build a home and then not have the means to support one. I therefore planned out my slender capital as carefully as I could. In the future my income must come from the products of the island: from rabbits, fish and the future farm. To produce most of my foodstuffs was the ideal to aim at, and to achieve as much independence as possible. The garden must be a large one. I must keep goats for milk and hens for eggs. Later I would be a shepherd as well, with a large flock of sheep to give both pleasure and profit.

I had already bought a young nanny goat, a pretty creature with a light-fawn coat, white feet below the knees, and face and ears daintily marked with white. This was Katherine, or Kitty for short; she was not expected to come into milking profit until next spring. Now I also obtained a young goat already in milk, naming her Matilda or Matty for short. Finally, there was a young billygoat to form the nucleus of the small flock of three or four milking goats which we would eventually content ourselves with. Matilda was of a darker fawn colour than Katherine, and Rufus, the billy, was of the colour that his name implied.

Of chickens Doris had charge of the flock destined to lead an island life. They were Rhode Islanders, headed by Jonathan, a noble cockerel with an unimpeachable pedigree. There were favourable reports forwarded to me of the hatching and rearing of this feathered community.

As to the garden, this had already been deeply dug over, and now waited to be set. Doris intended to put in the garden seeds herself, but I was not sure that I wanted her to come just yet, and to find nothing accomplished in house restoration.

We worked feverishly at the barn. Henry took entire charge of the culinary and house cleaning operations in the old dwelling. I taught him how to make bread and to cook generally, and he was soon adding flourishes of his own to the art. He read recipes secretly and brought some amazing, but mostly palatable, dishes to the table. The fare was simple enough. Fried bread and bacon for breakfast; vegetables, mostly swedes and potatoes, for dinner, with bully beef or tinned meat of some kind; for tea, toast, butter and jam, and on Sundays any cake Henry thought fit to surprise us with. At each meal mugs of tea helped to allay a thirst obtained by hard work. Just before bedtime, cocoa and toast was to be had by anyone who liked to get it himself. Sundays were holidays. Once a week, and sometimes once only in a fortnight, did we cross to the mainland for letters and more building material.

Beyond slates for the house roof, and lime for mortar, we had little heavy material to carry. New windows had to be made to order at a joinery, but the doors I built myself.

We had an excellent supply of oak from the wreck for lintels and beams. The brass bound wheel of the schooner we fixed in the breast of the chimney piece we had built in the barn. When this wheel was duly polished until the wood and brass shone, it was quite a resplendent sight under the lofty beams of this large room. Moreover, it was not to be a mere ornament. If one seized the spokes and swung the wheel four turns to starboard a chain came sliding down the chimney. It was an easy matter then to hook the kettle on for tea. When the kettle boiled, four turns of the wheel to port raised it off the fire. This was the great trick to play on visitors. Nonchalantly, Henry would swing the great wheel; and be delighted to see the stranger mystified by the movement of the kettle.

Early in April the barn was as far renovated as I intended it to be for the present, and we moved in wholesale from the house. My few items of furniture were easily accommodated in the new premises. We laid the great red foresail of the schooner over the floor, which was composed of wide, flat slabs of red island stone. The ship's tattered flags, her lifebuoys and some panelling, decorated and made bright the whitewashed walls. Opposite the wheel and chimney, at the other end of the room, we fixed the heavy, carved timber, decorated in white-and-black check, which once accompanied Alice on the schooner's bow. Above it, in the high apex window, the ship's binnacle and compass rested; to port and starboard respectively, in the corners of this end of the room, hung the ship's red port lamp and her green starboard one. Outside the door the ship's fog bell served as a musical knocker for visitors and a summons bell for meals, whilst her carved nameplate, torn from her bow by the sea, had been rescued and was now nailed forever on a conspicuous lower beam inside.

In this picturesque den we lived while we were repairing the dwelling house. We slept each on his own ship's cot, rescued from the wreck and newly sewn over with red sail canvas; and very comfortably we slept too. 'Barn' was a much too prosaic name for this living room, dominated by the dazzling brightness of the brass on the wheel, which Henry was under strict orders to keep shining. So henceforth it was called the 'Wheelhouse.'

When Doris came in April to plant her garden, Admiral – who, by the way, in case you have not already guessed this, is her father – came with her. We had whitewashed and decorated the one habitable little room in the old house for the distinguished lady visitor. For the first time also the table was spread in state in the Wheelhouse, a genuine tablecloth and china making a spotless display such as the old place had never known before. This, with a roaring fire of wreck coal and wood, was to welcome and warm the visitors after their cold voyage over a wind-whipped sea.

Zealously did Doris sow the garden with beans, peas, carrots, parsnips, and plant greens, rhubarb, shallots, currants and gooseberries, while I laid in the potato rows. Admiral, with his expert mastery of the joiner's craft, was not idle either. Together the three of us demolished the partition between the house-kitchen and the roofless room beside it, in order to work the will of Doris to have a larger kitchen. This partition proved to be nearly three feet thick and contained a chimney and fireplace which had been walled in at some time long past. The result was that when all the stones and mortar had been removed, Doris had a long, low-roofed kitchen for her delight, facing southwards to the shelter of the hill.

Those few days passed all too quickly. We were left alone once more. John and I now gave all our attention to the house, working steadily all day until five o'clock, when Henry would summon us to tea. After tea Henry

Ringing the Alice Williams bell outside the Wheelhouse

and John were free to enjoy themselves in the simple delights of sailing and fishing about the island in the *Storm Petrel*. John initiated Henry into the mysteries of lobster pot-making, and the results were not without profit to the island bill-of-fare. In turn we had lobster, crab, pollack, and later on mackerel, to vary the bully-beef menu.

The spring weather turned out to be ideal. For the whole month northerly winds prevailed, making the sea so calm in South Haven that the *Storm Petrel* was moored day and night on the tranquil water there.

The puffins returned late in March to the Sounds, and there was great excitement on the 3rd of April, when they finally made up their minds to land. This they did very suddenly and thoroughly at midday, flying inland by the hundred and occupying all their favourite positions on the high points, the rock outcrops and the stony hedge walls. There they jigged and bowed and laughed sonorously in their usual manner, for three hours, before flying away altogether. Two days later they again made a landing in force, and, as before, disappeared after a few hours. A bitter northeast wind, on April 16th, had the effect of driving them entirely away from the sea near the island, but they returned in thousands on the 18th, and the next day landed for the season.

The shearwaters, of course, had been here since February, and were now about to lay their solitary white egg in the recess at the end of a rabbit burrow. The storm petrels had only begun to arrive at night in the last few days of April.

April and May were, indeed, wonderful months for one who loved birds. Each day saw new visitors, quickly come and quickly gone. After the wheatears and chiffchaffs came the swallows and sand martins. Every day throughout April, May and early June swallows passed over the meadows, sometimes in hundreds, but more often by two's and three's, steadily from dawn until dusk. Then came willow wrens, swarming in the newly grown nettles and bramble bushes, olivaceous-coloured birds difficult to distinguish from the chiffchaffs at a distance, except when, at rare intervals, they paused to utter a few bars of song. But all these migrants were, as a rule, too restless and busy seeking food to have inclination to sing.

White wagtails on their way north, probably to Iceland and the Faroes, visited the island from March to mid-April, generally in small flocks of from a dozen to fifty. They came freely about the garden and buildings, causing a certain excitement to the pair of pied wagtails, their close relations, which had built a nest in an old wall near the Wheelhouse.

A few cuckoos called over the island, but were soon gone. Whitethroats were plentiful on some days, and late in April came the sleek, brown sedge warblers, swarming in the nettles as did the willow wrens. One pair remained to nest in the thicket of hemlock dropwort at the foot of the home meadow, where a spring runs down from the well. The male bird was the sweetest songster we had on the island that summer, and after singing all day would begin again at night as soon as the first incoming shearwater's cry disturbed his fitful sleep.

A few swifts, a few house martins, and many whinchats completed the list of April migrants. With May came spotted flycatchers, grasshopper warblers and turtle doves. Of larger birds there were occasional rooks, daws, common sand pipers and whimbrel, besides quite a long list of birds of which only one or two of its kind were noted.

After tea in the Wheelhouse it was our common practice to stand awhile at the windows looking out on the meadow. At this hour, after the cessation of the noise of building operations, the wild rabbits came out of their burrows to feed. They grazed and gambolled within a few yards of the Wheelhouse windows. Soon we learned to recognise individuals by certain peculiarities; for instance, one was particularly fat and large, another thin and lanky, one completely black, another with a white mark on its face, and one with its tail carried on one side, or, as John called it, 'hard-to-port.' It was amusing to watch the antics, flirtations and mimic battles of the bunnies. 'Hard-to-port' was a redoubtable warrior, and could perform the highest leap over an opponent's head. Rarely did rivals come to grips and lie scramming each other on the grass. They preferred to kick in passing and leap and dance around each other. The does tranquilly engaged in grazing all the time, their little ones darting timidly in and out of the burrows to snatch a bite of grass at intervals.

When a buzzard passed overhead there was a general crouching down, with ears laid flat. The little rabbits fled into their holes. The great black-backed gulls would walk about unconcernedly among the rabbits, and with the greatest cunning and affected indifference would edge closer and closer to a family group. At last, when near enough, the sharp, heavy beak would strike a young rabbit, there would be a pitiful scream, and away the gull would fly with its victim carried in its bill. These gulls fed largely on baby rabbits thus taken by stealth; and they slew puffins by patiently waiting at the mouths of the burrows for Mr Puffin to come out.

The windows framed pictures of the small birds, too. A pair of wheatears nested deep in a crevice in a bank opposite, and all day long carried grubs and flies to their hungry young. Spotted flycatchers, cuckoos and turtle doves perched on the bank at times – all welcome, if momentary, spring visitors.

One day, a very handsome and distinguished visitor settled on the bank in front of the window. It was a hoopoe, a brilliantly coloured bird not unlike a small jay, with a sulphur-tipped, fan-shaped head crest which it erected for a moment as it settled on the hedge bank. The hoopoe is a rare British bird, and this pretty fellow did not stay with us longer than one day. It flew about the island with that rising and falling method of flight, wings now closed and now widespread, adopted by woodpeckers.

Nearly all the visitors and non-breeding birds had left by the end of May. It was clear that the starlings did not intend to stay and nest in the summer. The flock gradually dwindled until but one pair was left, and even these two, after a thorough inspection of the old buildings, thought it best to fly away in the end.

I had never seen an ordinary house sparrow on the island until one day late in April a solitary cock arrived, worn out as if through the fatigue of a long flight. For two days it was too weak to chirp, but, presently, fattening on our table crumbs, it began to call incessantly. Of course there was no response – the nearest sparrows I knew of lived at Marloes – and at last Mr Sparrow flew away, no doubt despairing of colonising this lonely isle.

TEN

House building

WITH WHAT ZEAL did I attack the old dwelling house! The whole roof came off, almost to the last rafter and beam, so rotten and worm-eaten did we find the timbers. This work occupied us first, the intention being to put the roof on so that we could have a dry place to work under. Here the timbers from the wreck provided us with the necessary replacements; with wall plates, collars, main beams and rafters, mostly of old oak and pine. The few remaining Welsh-dug slates were taken off, and when the whole roof had been re-timbered I began putting on ordinary modern pale-grey asbestos slates, which, at a distance and from the mainland, give the appearance of a white roof, in keeping with the whitewashed walls of house and buildings. The roof was a fine vantage point, and as I worked I could survey my little kingdom, the countless thousands of my feathered subjects, and admire the acres of bluebells and thrift. The weather, as I have said, was exceedingly kind to us, and, had I but known, the haste to get the roof done first of all would not have been necessary, for we had no rain to speak of.

All the windows had to be renewed, and, except where they were of stone, new lintels put in above them. The two fireplaces also required lintels. Fortunately among the timbers rescued from the *Alice Williams* were a number of heavy oak beams, eight inches square, which had come from the captain's cabin and were in consequence nicely planed and finished. These I used for lintels and main supports. It was curious and interesting to discover that the old lintel, charred but still good, which I removed from the kitchen fireplace, was also a timber from a wooden sailing ship. In fact, it was of exactly the same width and thickness, and had the same finishing lines as the timber I replaced it with. I was therefore rebuilding the house on its old familiar lines. This charred lintel could not have come from an oak tree felled fewer than four hundred years ago.

The whole of the inside and outside walls of the house needed replastering, and at this work John proved himself very capable. The sandpit was dug deeply for a fine earth, the midden heap was sifted for the last ashes, and lime was added until we had a great mound of mortar for the purpose. The walls were scraped of loose plaster and earth and the work began. In this way most of the mason work fell to John, the carpentry to me.

New floors were required in all the rooms except the pantry and porch, where we left the red island flagstones as we found them. The wreck could not provide all the boards required for flooring, and we had to import some, as well as the boards for door-making. The doors I made, in my amateurish way, very plainly of straight boards and fixed lift-up latches to them. There would be no need for locks and keys in my home.

Another thing pleased me. I had no need to be too particular with my building operations; the house was already so quaintly built 'after a whimsical manner,' as Fenton, in his *Tour through Pembrokeshire* (1800), remarks, that my own improvements and unconventional methods could not but be somewhat in keeping with the inimitable style of the whole. Not one doorway, for instance, matches another: some are high and wide, some low and narrow, and some high and narrow. The windows vary in the same manner.

The floor of the kitchen I put down in concrete, tinted a warm red. A range was imported, one specially suitable for bread baking. The walls were plastered and whitewashed, and the first room was at last finished. Next, the pantry was fitted with a new north-facing window and with shelves, the walls whitewashed and the red flags scrubbed until they were a true red again. The guest room was refloored with flooring boards laid over joists consisting of the thick deck planks of the *Alice Williams*. The main room, when the anteroom partition had been knocked down and a new floor put across the timbers of the loft overhead, made an attractively large living room. The long, oak beams, cleaned of ages of dirt, were still straight and strong, so that we were saved the trouble of tearing the walls down to renew them. For a stairway to the loft we had the stepladder from the cabin of the wreck. The handrail from the schooner, too, when trimmed to required lengths, furnished me with the framing of the fireplace, which I had made rather spacious for burning logs and driftwood.

Alice Williams, you will see, had been most useful, saving much expense of material and the labour of ferrying it over. She had furnished me with timbers of such quality as I should scarcely have been able to afford. Nor do I forget that, apart from the house building, there were other directions in which she had been most useful. There were, for instance, innumerable items of use in boating, such as canvas, rope, wire, blocks, chains, tools, etc. Her freshwater tank, capable of holding 200 gallons, we set up for catching and storing precious rainwater from the house roof. The cook's galley we rolled laboriously across the meadows into one of the farm folds, and there I set it up to serve as a fowl house when Jonathan & Co. arrived. The other deckhouse was also rolled into a convenient place near the house.

Shortly after arriving on the island – the winter before – I had erected a short flagstaff on Spy Rock, one of the highest points on the island. Whenever we crossed to the mainland we ran up a flag (the Welsh dragon be it remarked) to warn the rabbit-dealer that we were coming over with a cargo for him. Now, in the summer, we used the flag to announce our crossing to anyone who might be waiting to meet us at Martynshaven.

The flagpole, however, was but a small one, merely an item that had drifted ashore on the island one day, and now that I had the tall topmast of the schooner I set about substituting this. Because of the convenience of having it near the house the topmast was erected on the 'Mountain,' as we facetiously called the protecting hillock behind the house. The Mountain is of a lower altitude than Spy Rock, but the extra height of the topmast made up for this.

Later, when the Welsh dragon had been torn to shreds by degrees in the perpetual breezes, Doris made a special flag for the island. How pleased were we when we first hoisted the new flag on the newly painted white topmast! There, spread to the breeze, on a field of green, bordered alternately black and white, danced three storm petrels, black with white rumps, flying towards the mast. The fluttering of the two tails of the long flag helped to create this illusion of actual flight. It was a masterpiece, this flag of ours.

The gulls had finished laying by now. No longer could Henry, who had developed a passion for their eggs fried in fat, collect them with safety. He had, however, put down a few hundred in pickle, which were to last him a few weeks at least. There were strict orders as to egg-collecting on the island. I allowed only the taking of eggs of the gulls, but of these in the season there had been more than enough for all of us. Nor did the collecting seem to interfere much with the number of young hatched by these gulls. They went on laying until the middle of June, at which time many were already hatched. In July the island bog was alive with young gulls.

For, incredible as it may seem, July did arrive, and found me putting the last touches to the interior of the home I had promised Doris, though there was much to be done still to the outside; a lot of pioneering still left for her to take part in.

ELEVEN

Promised lands

JULY THE TWELFTH proved a day of sunshine after many days of uncertain
weather and mist. There was a slight breeze from the southeast, so
that I was able to sail quietly northwards from the island, and across
St Bride's Bay to St Bride's Haven. Here, within a stone's throw of the
church, anchor was dropped and I went ashore to meet my bride.

St Bride's Church is prettily placed beside the sandy beach. There is no
village nearby, its sole neighbours being only a few scattered farms and
cottages, and on the hill to westward the high tower of St Bride's Castle.

When the ceremony was over, shortly after noon, our parents and sisters,
almost the sole witnesses of our quiet wedding, drank our health at the
feast held on the edge of the grass, after which we were free to sail away
alone together. It was almost the first time I had handled the boat without
John, but I was proud to be able to sail away in the bright, newly painted
Storm Petrel with my bride. Proudly did the infant engine start us on our

way, and then, when I hoisted sail, we sped away out into St Bride's Bay with a hissing wake of white foam behind us.

First of all Doris must needs view the home built for her, and to this end we sailed down for the island. But when we had passed through Jack Sound we met a heavy mist rolling up from the Atlantic. Some farmers, aware of the wedding, had assembled on the cliff near Jack Sound and now fired us a salute from their double barrels, and just before the mist enveloped us entirely.

The wind then dropped away, the sails napped idly, and the mist thickened until we could see no more than a few yards before us. Some shearwaters, those mist- and fog-loving birds, began to pass us in the Broad Sound, skimming without apparent effort, now showing their white breasts and now their black upper parts; first with the left wing tip almost touching the sea and then the right wing tip, in a movement that reminded you of the right and left swing of a skater.

As we drew closer to our island home, steering entirely by compass, the numbers of puffins, gulls, razorbills and guillemots resting on the water increased until we were soon forging through large flocks of birds. And so we sailed till at last we caught the faint, intermittent blast of the fog signal from the lighthouse: then the wash of sea upon rocks; and so in deep mist we entered the South Haven of our island home.

Among many of the Lands Promised to Doris, Grassholm was first and foremost. We were to have a honeymoon on Grassholm; we were to be the first honeymooners on that lonely Atlantic isle. Long ago I had promised her this, in a valorous moment when all things seemed easy to achieve if she so wished. And now the wedding was over and the bride ready for the honeymoon. I therefore asked her to pray for a northerly wind if she still wished to sail there.

While the wind stayed in the south we sailed elsewhere, taking a fair breeze where it blew us. Thus, the day after the wedding found us sailing before a mild sou'wester on the calm waters of Milford Haven and that evening found us drifting with the tide in the wooded reaches of the

Cleddau, listening to hooting owl and reeling nightjar.

The hoped-for wind came stealing out of the north two days later and found us at the port of Martynshaven, whither we had sailed the previous evening. The wind was true north and blowing steadily, the morning was full of sunshine, and our hearts full of morning happiness. 'To sea! To sea!' was the cry. 'Where e'er the wind will blow us!'

One by one, the Marloes fishermen were putting out to sea, and, when we had scraped together all the provisions we could find, and filled a large can with water, we set forth too. There was a merry 'Altogether-heave-ho!' as we together launched our strong craft; then 'Jump in and stand by with the boat hook.' For the sea was breaking choppily on Martynshaven beach, the north wind blowing upon this north-facing beach. A short pull-off with oars was necessary before the infant engine was set to work.

Northwards we pointed her while we trimmed our vessel, making all snug and secure in case we encountered choppy seas. Then did I hoist sail; first the wide, white lug, then the white jib upon the improvised bowsprit. The *Storm Petrel* sprang forward to their urge, pointing due west, and we sailed away north of Skomer for the far Isle of Grassholm, crossing the north-streaming tide above Jack Sound and past the Garland Stone of Skomer.

Fishermen bending their backs over oars and lobster pots in the shelter of Skomer cliffs, must have seen the full beauty of the *Storm Petrel* as she lay over to the brisk northerly breeze, sailing out to sea on the last of the northern stream. Her white freeboard danced merrily in harmony with the white-capped wavelets of tide and wind-whipped sea, her stem parted the water with an eager, smiting sound, and the song of her rushing, eddying wake soothed the uproar of the noisy Infant, as we called the boat's engine. The breeze was so good when we got out into the open sea beyond Skomer that we silenced the Infant and rushed on to the pleasant murmur of slapping waves and sails close-filled with the favouring wind.

After all, the *Storm Petrel* was but a small craft to be sailing Atlantic seas, and I must confess that, at first, I had some qualms about venturing across the tide races to a harbourless islet.

The *Storm Petrel* was but seventeen feet long by five and a half of beam, and carried a pocket engine of a strength equal to two men rowing. She was prettily painted in white with red fender. With her two white sails out on her white mast and Doris at the tiller, I was content to sail on forever. I cared not for a bigger boat – this was the boat for us, a boat that could sail in and out of sounds and creeks, lie upon tiny beaches, and be hauled out of the water without extra hands. Give me a small boat for summer sailing, and one that has a small engine to do the hardest work. A small engine, too, has these advantages: it is simple and costs little to run, and does not go too fast to spoil the pleasure of sailing; yet when the breeze is faint the engine will drive the ship forward, creating more wind to help fill the idle sails.

The tall cliffs of Skomer slowly faded behind us, and southward that faraway isle of ours – the red land of the Lower Island – vanished in the mist. Nearer and nearer loomed the green shore of Grassholm, famed, among other things, for its colony of gannets; for here dwells the only colony of these birds in all England and Wales. There are a few others in Scotland and Ireland, and though they bred formerly on Lundy Island, fate or mankind has extirpated them there.

The fishermen of Marloes were wont, in the past summers of the nineteenth century, to fish for shellfish about the fertile shores of this islet. Now, so they will tell you, the weather is never continuously fine enough for them to risk such a venture. They have left the islet to the birds, and the gannets have profited thereby, increasing year by year in number.

Many are the tales the Marloes men can relate to you, if you lend a sympathetic ear, but you must wait on the greybeards, who alone can speak from their own experience and that of their forbears. There are tales of boats lost at moorings there in times of sudden ground swells, of marooned men, and of thrilling rescues; but there is no story of gentle times and faithful winds. All these are forgotten in the memories of hard times, rough living and stormy days there, and of too fair breezes that drove the fishermen under reefed sail headlong to refuge in Dale, or Martynshaven. So this is the first tale of the sea's good nature and the wind's fairness to the

Marloes fisherman with lobster pots

first honeymoon on Grassholm. I should say, the first human honeymoon, remembering the gannets which enact their ridiculous love antics there in the spring.

These birds flew in hundreds above and about us as we sailed in towards the green shores of Graesholm, to give it an ancient Scandinavian title, meaning the 'Green Islet.' We were approaching the east side, which is pleasantly green with long grass; the west side is snowy white with thousands of gannets. There are no havens, harbours, or beaches at Grassholm, only two or three narrow gashes in the rocks wide enough to allow a boat to enter and be moored safely, always provided there is no ground swell. The smallest ground sea, as I found on another occasion, will roll in from the open sea and in less than a few minutes is capable of smashing any boat moored between the narrow rock walls.

On this occasion the winds were kind to us and brought us fair weather, so that we were able to moor the *Storm Petrel* in the calm water of the southernmost gut in the low cliffs. Then we scrambled ashore with the same sort of feeling as Columbus must have had when he scrambled ashore upon a western coast.

You might have thought that we should have at once rushed around the island sightseeing, eager especially to examine the gannet colony, which, although out of sight of this quiet little landing place in the rocks, assailed our ears with its uproar; a sound marvellously akin to the combined whirr of a dozen hay-cutting machines. The stench attacked our nostrils, and all the while a faint airy shower of the moulted white down from the young birds came eddying and dancing about us, borne by the north wind from the far end of this remote bird sanctuary.

No, we were wiser from much experience that told us hunger is no companion in the tranquil enjoyment of undiscovered lands. The two hours' sail in the boat and the task of mooring her off, added to the keenness of the north wind and our natural appetites, had made us really hungry. So we sat down in the warm sunshine, under the lee of the cliffs, and ate and drank.

'How long do we stay here?'

'That depends on the weather, and on how long you want to stay.' 'I was thinking of our water supply. At the rate we are drinking we shall be waterless by tonight.'

'There's supposed to be water here somewhere. We'll have a grand search presently. Meanwhile, I'm consumed with thirst – it must be excitement and salt air – I hope you are thirsty too, because you must drink cup for cup with me. All marooned adventurers do.'

When we were replete we packed up our stores and put them out of the hot sunshine behind a cool rock. From where we sat basking under the low cliff we could watch a group of seals also basking on some seaweed-covered rocks at the edge of the tide below us. The seals were singing a dirge among themselves, and every now and then the biggest of them, lying on the top of the rock, would raise his head (and his tail as well, to balance his head as he lay on his side) to utter a louder, musical moan that would start the others into renewed lamentations. The burden of their song would seem to be heavy with lament; a dirge of the sea, yet pleasantly musical to the ordinary ear.

TWELVE

The lesser islands

To DESCRIBE THE WONDER of the gannet colony requires a powerful pen and a command of many choice superlatives. The whole upper cliff of the island's northwest corner, wherever there is foothold for a nest, is covered with the homes of these birds. As it was mid-July, the nests were occupied by young birds, mostly in the pure white downiness of extreme youth. A few nests contained a solitary egg, whilst a few had advanced in the other direction, and contained young already moulting their down tor the first speckled plumage of adolescence. The gannet lays but one egg, rears but one young in the year, and the young gannet does not get its full white plumage until its third or fourth year.

As we approached the outskirts of the colony the uproar increased. The nests, so many hummocks of flattened seaweed and grass, plus trampled guano, were about three feet apart. On each hummock or pedestal sat a young bird with one parent brooding over it. Overhead flew thousands of other adults, their great white bodies filling the air like giant snowflakes. The adults deserted their babies as we came within touching distance, and floundered away headlong from us in a confused mass. Beating their wings wildly, they endeavoured to rise up into the already overcrowded air. Their long wings, threshing over the ground, dealt many of the patient nestlings a staggering blow.

On being displaced from their pedestals, the young ones would hasten to get back, and by digging their beaks into the sides or tops of the nests, they usually managed to haul themselves up again. They quarrelled fiercely with each other if they happened to meet, and there was a rare set-to if one happened to mount on to the pedestal of another. They used their beaks freely until one or the other had been thrown overboard, king-of-the-castle fashion.

Their method of defence against human beings – or it may have been merely fear – appeared to take the form of disgorging their last meal in front of us, and in pecking, at approach, arms and legs. Often they would throw up whole a freshly swallowed herring, mackerel or pollack, and as we passed through the colony a trail of every kind of local fish was left in our wake by indignant nestlings, as well as by some of the adults.

It was not easy to estimate the size of this great colony, but there were probably four thousand nests covering a couple of acres of sloping cliff.

The uproar was deafening, and the stench, made up of the odours of dead fish, rotten seaweed, manure, and occasional dead birds – the whole encouraged by a warm sun – was well-nigh unendurable.

We left the colony and continued our exploration round the island, leisurely pointing out the beauties to each other, but carefully looking for a spring or well to renew our water supply.

The eastern side of Grassholm was pleasantly quiet after the turmoil of the gannetry. One may rest here, in soft, long green grass, and listen to the gentle tinkle of the rock pipits and the murmur of the swift tide as it runs past over the shallow ground and rocks half-awash below you. Here, safe from the more cruel storms from south and west, you may build your hermit's hut and live in a pleasant solitude. For company you will have the birds, the seals, a few flowers, and there is room for a large garden in the deep, peaty soil.

Such was my idle reverie as we basked in the sunshine on the soft couch of grass of that quiet eastern side, looking out towards the far mainland, Skomer and our own island.

Grassholm is no more than twenty-two acres all told, but is so uneven that it appears larger. The sea birds crowd its western cliffs chiefly, and besides the gannets there are hundreds or guillemots, razorbills and kittiwakes. There are only one or two puffins and a few black-backed and herring gulls. These, with one pair of oystercatchers, a shag and some rock pipits were all the birds we saw. Seals are very numerous, and will entertain you with their songs if you can steal upon them unawares in the creeks. To count twenty or thirty seals lying along the edge of the rocks by the tide was a common occurrence.

We found water eventually, a mere drip tip-tapping from under a ledge of rock; and when we had gathered a tinful we found that even this was brackish. It was guaranteed to cure the thirsty and to take away all desire to drink from the merely moderately thirsty. Perhaps it would be quite palatable when boiled and cooled again. As it was it savoured of much salt and alas, of gannets, though this last flavour may have been owing to the ever-present effluvium of the gannetry which refused to leave us entirely in any part of the island.

From the highest point we watched the rich colours of the sunset foretell for us continuance of the gods' favours. The thousand flying bodies of the gannets took on a rosy hue as they moved through the coloured air. Effortless on the gentle breeze, the long, black-tipped wings of the birds sustained their white bodies without quivering; only the long, pointed white tail moved as it steered the course, now up, now down, and now to one side. Groups of gannets flew out to sea upon fresh fishing adventures, and long lines and parties of returning birds came in with their harvest, already swallowed; for the young gannet helps himself from the parental gullet by inserting his beak therein, and is not fed with clean fish straight from the sea, as are most sea birds.

Below us, below the seething gannetry, the tide was roaring from east and west northwards, for the northern stream strikes upon the south point of Grassholm and divides into two streams, which run along the east and west coasts to unite again at some point north of the island. One might well imagine Grassholm as a pebble dropped in midstream of some great river and lying half awash, while the current streams furiously on each side of it; such is the strength of the spring tides there.

The colours lingered about the northern horizon during the starry night. The full moon bathed us in light as we slept in the warm grass on the eastern slopes. Very little did we sleep, for youth and life were both combined with magic circumstance in keeping us wide awake to the beauty of the July moon, the sounds of the hurrying tide, the eerie cry of bird and moan of seal. Ever and anon I roused myself to listen more acutely to the tune of the sea, and to test the direction of the wind; but all night long the north wind soughed and sighed, saying, 'It is well, I blow softly; no other wind dares me. Sleep thou, thy boat is safe, the moorings are listless in the calm water.' For all I cared about was that the wind would stay immovable in the north all night, and thus keep our boat safe; for if the wind backed, who knew what swell or storm might rise in the night from the south?

Among other considerations, the lack of water was the chief reason for abandoning Grassholm on the following day. It was, therefore, agreed that we set sail for Ramsey Island at high water, while the northern stream had yet three hours to run, and so to help us northwards to that lofty island. So we bade adieu to Grassholm and her gannets with regret, but with added eagerness to explore the new Lands of Ramsey, the Bishops and the Clerks.

In exactly three hours of nice sailing we arrived at Ramsey south harbour, and spent two days in this pleasant land, thanks to the hospitality of the resident farmer. In return, as he was interested in birds, we advised him that the 'big buzzard' he spoke of as haunting the island hills was really a golden eagle; the only one wild in all England and Wales. There was no mistaking the great bird's sweeping pinions, its size, and its shrill bark. I knew also that a pair of eagles had been set free many years ago on Skomer, and that this was, doubtless, the survivor. Ramsey has many rare and interesting birds and flowers, while her west coast is haunted by many seals.

But the time when we could thus idly cruise about from place to place was drawing to a close, for a return to work on our own island was becoming necessary. Therefore, bidding our host and hostess goodbye, we launched our boat and set out.

Even after so short a parting from the *Storm Petrel* as two days, it was good to be once more upon a tide, liable to further wandering and adventure. The thought of the long cruise home filled us with pleasure. After all, an island home is a perennial delight to return to after the smallest absence.

The wind was still in the north: a fresh morning breeze which would die away and dwindle around the northern compass with the sun. We had promised ourselves a visit to all the Bishops and Clerks, those tide-harried rocks out to sea west of Ramsey, and that is why we first pointed north up Ramsey Sound, taking the last of the northern stream to carry us to the North Bishop.

The wind being east of north, as soon as we had passed out of the northern mouth of the Sound, we turned northwest for our first destination and hoisted all our canvas to help.

The tides run very strongly about the maze of Bishops and Clerks rocks. When we came up under the lee of the tall North Bishop the current was just beginning to run south. We ran into a tiny creek in the cliff out of the way of the stream, and tied the *Storm Petrel* to the rocks, letting her gently rub her fenders against the cliff as the slight backwash from the current rocked her.

Thus, we claim to be of the enterprising few who have landed on this lonely rock, and, in accordance with tradition which rules there, we added each our stone to the small cairn which marks the summit.

When you see a pile of stones on an eminence in deserted lands you may know the traditional ceremony at a glance. But we also removed a stone and carried it away with us for the very good reason that we required an anchor; having realised that it is better to anchor off in these places than to moor alongside, no matter how calm the anchorage or moorings. It saves paint, if not the more serious wear and tear to the wood.

The North Bishop comprises a chain of rocks in a straight line from sou'west to nor'east. The links are separated at high water by the tide, which rushes through with great force. I suppose, really, that the one high rock is the Bishop, and the rest of them are his satellites or Clerks, attending him all in a row. One or two Clerks have strolled away on errands and got caught in the tide halfway to St David's or to Ramsey, or have wandered away towards the other Bishops, whom they may possibly serve. You may imagine one Bishop sending a messenger to another, for altogether there are four lofty, green-pated Bishops: first, my lord the North (or should he be the Arch Bishop?), then the Middle Bishop, the Little Bishop and finally the South Bishop.

Undoubtedly the finest fellow, and most closely followed by his retinue of Clerks, is the North Bishop, which we had the honour to visit. Here resort many seafowl to rear their young, particularly guillemots, razorbills and black-backed gulls. Seals attend, as everywhere here, and mallows grow in the sheltered niches of the rocks. The grass is long, wiry and slippery to the feet, and the whole place is much like a miniature Grassholm save in shape. There are, of course, no gannets, and the shape of this Bishop is thin and narrow – an ascetic fellow.

The Middle Bishop, to which we next set sail, is small, plump and well attended with acolytes and Clerks. As far as we could see he is much like his Northern brother in having the same flora and fauna, and the same cruel tides. As we struck upon the north side, down which the current was pouring in a southwest direction, we had difficulty in finding a tideless anchorage. The *Storm Petrel* could not stem the tide to work around to the south side and so seek a harbour there. We put in to one creek we found, but even here the tide was sneaking quietly through a crevice to the other side, and kept dragging us into the crack as soon as we shut off power.

Now I wished to land Doris at all the Bishops, but particularly at the South Bishop; for we both wished to visit the lighthouse there.

'You see here,' I explained in my best guidebook manner, pointing to the green head of the Middle Bishop looming above us as we lay under his bird-strewn cliff, 'a similar construction to the North Bishop, and occupied by seafowl of a similar kind. In fact, it is entirely similar, if smaller and less well known. Obviously, no one except shipwrecked people have ever landed here, for there is no cairn or sign of human hand. I propose we go ahead with the tide and visit the other two Bishops if we can, ere taking the last of the tide home. We'll try for the Little Bishop first.'

So we set out again, drifting into the roaring tide off this Middle Bishop. Unhappy mariners, untimely driven in rough weather, masters of ketches and schooners, know well the wicked ferocity of the currents that sweep south from the Bishops over foul ground.

We experienced these for the first time that day in our little ship, and though the day was calm, and a gentle zephyr smoothing along with the tide, the current nevertheless lifted, heaved, dipped and boiled as if a gale were a-blowing. Through this the *Storm Petrel* bumped her way. The stream ran straight for the South Bishop, and had we wished to visit the Little Bishop we could scarcely have done so save by first preparing a plan to creep along the Middle Bishop shore, make a sharp tack to eastward, and fall back upon the Little Bishop with the tide. As it was, we were unprepared, and finding ourselves in so good and true a course for the lighthouse, we gave the Little Bishop the cold shoulder. Poor forlorn fellow, there he lies, an out-at-heel dwarf, scarcely a Clerk to attend him, lonely like his greater neighbour, the South Bishop.

With all her canvas set and with a favouring breeze on her starboard from the north, with engine and with tide the good ship fairly raced towards the rock on which the lighthouse is perched. We got free from the worst of the heave when half a mile away from the Middle Bishop, and the *Storm Petrel* settled down to sail in a steady, yacht-like manner.

As we drew nearer and nearer we could make out the steps of the landing place, and could see the three figures of the lighthousemen watching and waiting for us. It was quite a proud moment for us, for was not the *Storm Petrel* racing in all her loveliness before critical eyes? Also, we were bringing news (we had remembered to commandeer a newspaper for them from Ramsey house), and it was also an opportunity for them to post letters. Therefore they were welcoming us fervently, if for selfish reasons.

The tide does not forget the South Bishop. It was nearly low water, and the current at its strongest of spring tide, but with the speed she had upon her the boat could defeat the stream. I hauled in the jib, then the lug, and unstepped the mast while Doris steered us through the tide into the small haven beside the steps.

All the conveniences for mooring a small boat obtain at the South Bishop, and in a few minutes we were climbing a rope ladder ashore, after the *Storm Petrel* had been moored off by an overhead cable stretched from cliff to cliff across the tiny haven. The lighthouse is perched on the summit of this tall and substantial rock, and an ascent is made by flights of steps cut out of the solid cliff.

There was something weighing upon the lightkeepers' minds. This was clear as soon as we had introduced ourselves. The young supernumerary officer, whom I had met on my own island, introduced us to the chief and second officers, in all seriousness, 'Mr and Mrs Lockley . . . on their honeymoon!' The ground thus broken, the supernumerary produced from his breast pocket, as we were only halfway up the steps to the lighthouse, a treasured letter, and in a deprecatory, apologetic manner, said –

'Would you. . . could you. . . do you mind posting this letter for me when you get back ashore, please?'

As if by magic, these words by the supernumerary caused the right hands of the chief and second officers to visit their own breast pockets and to produce each a letter, all sealed and stamped ready.

'And if you please, this little letter, when you can find time to post it?'

'Do you mind. . . just this one as well?'

This was what had been troubling them probably ever since their keen eyes had seen our sail leaving Ramsey Sound early in the morning: the great problem of getting a letter to loved ones ashore; and this now in a fair way to be accomplished, their minds were carefree again, and they were ready to extend to us the utmost hospitality.

We were piloted over the spotlessly clean and shining rooms of the lighthouse, from the dazzling lantern room to the shed where are housed the fog signal engines. Everything was in perfect order and it was clear that life here is one monotonous round of routine and watch, varied by spells of fog and mist, when extra work and appalling noise is occasioned by the engines driving compressed air for the booming siren. The sea might be calm or rough, the wind soft or loud, but routine goes on and on, as regular and as constant as the interminable smell of paraffin that clings to all lighthouses.

Of course there are days when the Relief is due, and a month ashore hoped for, weather permitting the boat to come. If you are something of a bird-lover, you can study the hundreds of birds which, dazzled by the powerful white light, call there to rest upon the bird ladders which have been provided by a very humane Royal Society for the Protection of Birds. But it was not now the migration season, and the place was deserted save for a stray pigeon and a few rock pipits. Mallows grow here in the scanty grass, but there is little soil for gardening. We were further told that nothing would grow in any case owing to the millions of rock lice and earwigs that swarm everywhere after dark.

In the warm kitchen we were entertained to tea. The ancient visitors' book we signed had its first entry dated 1854. In return for their hospitality we left them some fresh milk and fruit, and the newspaper.

As we were about to step aboard our ship, homeward bound, the second officer tentatively remarked, 'If you should possibly be this way again, you will remember us and call for . . . letters?'

The others silently concurred with this reminder.

We cast off, drifted into the angry tide race beyond the Rock, and into a wind which was now dead fair, sailing onward across the smooth sea for home in the late afternoon sunshine. Running before the breeze the sun was very warm upon our uncovered heads, and the tide served well.

Safely home at Skokholm, Storm Petrel
back on her berth

What hurry was there to reach home? I headed her for the mainland lodge, eleven miles across the bay, stopped the noisy Infant and let the *Storm Petrel* go her quiet way.

The stem parted the water with a gentle lapping which made us drowsy, so, turn and turn about, we slept and steered, lying blissfully on the sun-warmed boards.

These voyages were the first of many such in this and in succeeding summers.

THIRTEEN

We entertain

OUR ISLAND WAS NEVER SO overcrowded with human beings as when, on a day in August, a cricket match was played in the north meadow. It came about through the issue of a challenge by mainland friends, to some of whom we owed much for hospitality and willing help in the past. It was our opportunity to repay some of this hospitality by inviting them to play the match on the island, and they accepted gladly. Though the thought of the sea journey caused the ladies of the party to shake their heads, they were very eager to have had the experience, and to see what manner of place it was that Doris and I were content to dwell in.

On our part we were not sure of raising a full team, but in the end, with the assistance of visitors, the three lightkeepers and John, we raised the required eleven. A calm day was essential to the success of the party, and in any case the mainlanders would not brave a breeze on the water. Therefore, when the first day of flat calm arrived we sailed over at sunrise,

John and I, to fetch the opposing team.

At 9.30 a.m. Martynshaven beach was the scene of considerable excitement, as both *Storm Petrel* and *Foxtrot* were loaded with a burden of ten men and four ladies (comprising the eleven members of the opposing team, John, a visitor to the island, and myself). The ladies, all four very young, with natural sunburn and roses on their cheeks, occupied the place of honour in the *Storm Petrel*. John was in charge of the *Foxtrot*, with its cargo of young men, and the cricketing outfit.

The *Storm Petrel* took the *Foxtrot* in tow at the end of a length of rope. Jack Sound, almost rippleless at the slack of tide, caused wonder in the minds of those who thought only of its reputation for wrecks and rough seas. Halfway across the Broad Sound a little breeze sprang up, and John instantly hoisted sail so that the *Foxtrot* began to run down upon the *Storm Petrel*. To remedy this I hoisted sail too.

The two boats entered South Haven under full sail yet connected by the tow rope. A few yards behind us swam a seal, prompted no doubt by curiosity.

South Haven was gaily decorated with every flag and piece of bunting the busy island team had been able to lay hands on. At the top of the landing steps Edward, the donkey, was ready, harnessed to the trucks, both donkey and trucks dressed with flowers and lofty plumes of bracken. The first item in the day's programme was a march to inspect the lighthouse. Edward was there to draw the ladies in the decorated trucks along the tramline which runs from landing to lighthouse, a mile-long, uphill journey.

The lighthouse aroused much admiration in those who had never seen over one. One comment of 'Why, I thought there was only a hut with a bit of wick in it!' was surprising, coming as it did from folk who live on a coast bristling with lighthouses.

The journey back to the farmhouse, when the trucks loaded with the whole party were let go at full speed down the incline (Edward remaining behind, his services dispensed with), was filled with screams and laughter. The last mad rush downhill was braked to a standstill by a careful lighthouse-keeper, and the party found themselves in the home meadow.

The island flag waved gently from the flagstaff on the hill above the house; and on the grassy lawn below, under streams of bunting, lunch was waiting the hungry folk. Exactly twenty-two people sat down to eat, this being probably the largest population ever assembled at the old house.

The island team was anxious to get a practice in before the match started. No one knew where our bowling or batting talent lay, while all modestly protested their incompetence. In the end we put up a good fight against the Marloes folk. Marloes was represented by four ladies, five men and two boys, we by five ladies and six men, but while Marloes had been practising for the event, we had had no opportunity.

On a high plateau of closely grazed meadow stumps were pitched. This ground had an additional advantage in that spectators and fielders commanded a wide and interesting view of the Broad Sound and the mainland, and all the traffic on the sea about the island, from Grassholm in the west to Linney Head in the southeast. Some trawlers that passed gave a friendly hoot on seeing so many white-clad figures on a lonely island. The incident that caused us the most amusement, however, was the running aground of a ketch that came in too close to the shore. The helmsman, evidently anxious to see what was afoot on the island, sailed in close to the Stack, and with his eyes too much on the cricket match, ran dead on to the seaweed-covered Tidball Rock near the Stack. As it was but an hour before low water of spring tide, there the ketch had to remain for two hours until the tide floated her off. On first striking we saw them hasten to lower the ship's boat and try to tow the vessel off. Quite in vain, however. Luckily the rock was soft with the summer growth of weed and the sea smooth. So all the crew could do for two hours was to watch the match!

The islanders batted first and were all out for forty-six. Then the mainlanders went in. We disposed of seven wickets for twenty runs, but their first man was still at the wicket, and he proved to be our greatest difficulty and finally our undoing. At last, with the score at forty-one he was caught out, and the remaining batsmen only raised the score to fifty-three. The Lower Island lost by seven runs.

Before tea there was a bathing regatta in South Haven, where the two boats were moored side by side. After tea, on the grass as before, there were competitive games, and stunts with poles and pennies. Finally, before leaving the island, the mainlanders must needs see the creek where the *Alice Williams* had been wrecked, and inspect the store of coal and timber she had given us. Alice herself, newly painted, they had already seen on first entering South Haven, where she forever occupies a proud position on a rock overlooking the sea, her wooden body firmly bolted in that leaning position she so loved to affect in her seafaring days.

Towards sunset a move was made to the boats. Some young voices demanded to be allowed to stay the night in order to hear the 'cuckles and cock-lollies,' as the shearwaters are locally termed. They were overruled, and presently both boats were sailing back for the mainland before a faint westerly breeze. Some last red flares were fired from boat and from island, as goodbye signals, ere the boats turned the corner of the haven out of sight of the islanders, who were waving and cheering so frantically from the landing steps.

Long before the Marloes men have finished making their pots, the hardy Frenchmen are to be seen on the coasts, in February, even in January. These little Breton smacks, so variously coloured as to hull and sails, are well known in every haven from Penzance to Fishguard and along the Irish coast. They are after the crayfish – *la langouste* of the French epicure. Here the Bretons come, ostensibly, to fish on the shoals about the lonely Smalls lighthouse, more than twelve miles at sea. They may not legally fish within the three-mile limit of any shore or island; nevertheless, if there is no Fishery Protection vessel about, they freely drop their baited cages along some favourite shore.

One misty day late in April, when we set sail by compass for isolated, uninhabited Grassholm, which lies halfway between us and the Smalls, we pierced the fog about the islet to find a startled Frenchman in the midst of his illegal work. There he was, hauling his cages, *cases* he calls them, cylindrical affairs three feet long by two feet diameter, made of battens and string netting, weighted each with two of the speckled stones of Camaret, and baited with gurnet. Two cages are dropped on one rope, which is buoyed with painted corks.

There were at least twenty separate buoy ropes bobbing to the northerly breeze along the south shore of Grassholm, apart from the cages which had already been hauled and stacked by two of the crew working in the ship's dinghy. The smack was dodging to and fro with foresheet to windward, waiting for the dinghy to return the cages on board.

Seeing their bewilderment and hesitation, we ran the newly painted *Storm Petrel* alongside their little boat, and putting on a peak cap I cried: 'Pourquoi pêchez-vous ici? C'est défendu.'

It had been better if I had spoken in Welsh, which is nearer akin to the Breton language than French itself.

Doris immediately destroyed the illusion of authority by smiling engagingly and saying: 'Bonjour.'

The two fishermen, in their blue smocks, yellow oilskin aprons, red berets and wooden clogs, only grinned, shaking their heads to signify to me that they did not, or would not, understand my question. In a few moments they were piling enormous crabs into our boat as offerings of peace and conciliation.

We took them in tow and motored across to the smack. Homemade wine, biscuits and tobacco were pressed on us. The conversation consisted of a mixture of dockyard English, schoolday French and gesticulation. When we left, after taking our turn at the great tiller of the smack, we were piled high with crabs, cases, bottles of wine, and other gifts which they insisted we must take. And we were invited to sail with them to Brest, whenever we desired a holiday in Brittany.

While we landed on Grassholm and saw that all was well with the gannet colony, which we felt to be under our care, the Frenchmen returned to their fishing, anxious to finish their haul before the current changed. It was pleasant to lie in the long dead grass, eating lunch, enjoying the misty sunshine, and watching the beautiful response of the smack to the skilful helmsmanship of the Breton men.

One windy day late in June we again had the opportunity of watching this seamanship. French smacks, red, white, green, blue and black, one after another came flying past Skokholm, driven by a stiff westerly breeze from the Smalls, seeking the shelter of Milford Haven. We could recognise the boat of our friend – Le Capitaine – by her green-and-white hull. With the glass we could read the names of the smacks: Belle de Nuit, Belle de Jour, Yvette, Colbert, Cygne – all enchanting names.

Suddenly our friend's boat came about, and leaving the procession slanted towards our shore. Another followed her, and by a series of tacks both presently gained the shelter of our harbour, coming very nicely into South Haven against a head wind. They had no idea of the depth of our water, but each time as they came about the leadsman sounded and chanted the measure aloud, until at last they were snug inside our haven, with anchor and sheet down, and soon all stowed – a charming picture.

As part of our hospitality to the two crews, each of six men, we taught them to play cricket in the home meadow. They had not the remotest idea of the game, but they soon learnt, and after the first lesson were wildly enthusiastic. When the lightkeepers joined in we numbered nearly a full field. They stayed three days, coming ashore each afternoon and evening to play the wonderful new game.

At last the weather became warm and calm, and the tide so suitable for fishing that they were reluctantly compelled to bid us farewell. On the last day we gave them a tea party. Each man, as he entered the house, removed his beret and left his clogs in the porch. Last of all entered the two *petits mousses*, the rosy-cheeked apprentices, shy urchins of ten years of age, already able to handle a smack, who ate their cakes in awed silence, gazing at a frieze which Doris had painted on the wall. Their clogs looked very tiny beside those of the captain's in that row of twenty-four beside our doormat.

FOURTEEN

The story of the shearwater

S O LITTLE RELIABLE INFORMATION on the habits of the manx shearwater could we find in our bird books that we determined to discover the birds' life story for ourselves, in as far as the periods of incubation and fledging time were concerned.

We knew already that the shearwater arrived very early in the year on the island. In an observation of three years we found that it arrived regularly sometime early in February, but it was not until mid-March that these birds began to call each night in any number. From that time onwards until the middle of August they screamed each night over the house, as they passed to and from their nests in the rabbit holes. Their strange note I have already described.

Late during the day the shearwaters begin to come in towards the island from the far open sea. One by one they collect until sometimes there are thousands in a flock. They sweep up towards the island from the Bristol Channel. If the weather is misty they arrive in the vicinity of the two islands, Skomer and this island, where they breed, some hours before dark, but in clear weather they may not appear until dusk. Other birds, perhaps from St George's Channel and northwards, converge upon the islands from the west, and still others sweep down St Bride's Bay from the north.

However numerous they may be on the sea near the island, they do not land until two hours after sunset, and they may be later if there is a clear sky, or if the moon is shining. The birds do not like the moon, and are much less noisy in moonlight. The darker and stormier the night, with plenty of wind and rain, the more they revel in it, and the more they scream.

At the appointed time one may confidently expect to hear the scream of the first bird venturing inland, and in a few minutes there will be hundreds more screaming; then, if you go out of doors, you can hear the swish of their wings as they glide past you at a terrific speed.

It is strange that these swift-flying birds can suddenly check their flight and drop with perfect accuracy in the dark upon their chosen rabbit hole, even where that hole is amongst the crowded entrances and exits of a rabbit warren. It is, however, just as well that the bird can do this, for the shearwater is a very indifferent traveller on land, progressing by means of a series of short little runs on its toes. It cannot balance itself when stationary, but has to rest flat on its breast, its legs being placed rather far back on its body. On rough ground it scrambles along by using its half-outspread wings and pushing with its feet.

How do the shearwaters know each his own rabbit hole? And how, in the first place, do they find one to suit them? I suppose the old birds know where to go from past experience, and apparently they have exceptionally keen eyesight or instinct in the dark. I have seen a pair home hunting in the spring, exploring the holes and crannies along the foot of a hedge. They find out the most isolated and hidden burrows as well as the crowded warrens. We found that each year the same pairs returned to the same holes, so that, in spite of all their wide wanderings over the Atlantic in mid-winter, the majority pair for life.

A wing that flew from Venice to Skokholm

The foot of the shearwater spread over the egg, showing the broad webbing below the sharp keeled leg

The nest is made in the recess at the end of a burrow, no matter if the burrow is many yards long and far from the surface, or if it is only a blind shaft a few feet long. The shearwater collects whatever it can find in or near the burrow to make a lining for the nest, such as dried grass, dead bracken fragments, and rootlets torn from the walls of the burrow. Here it lays its solitary white egg sometime in May, or late in April.

We found that before the egg was laid the parents were very irregular in their sojourns by day at the nest. Sometimes one bird would stay, sometimes the other, often both or neither. Each dark night they would meet together at the mouth of the burrow and indulge in amorous billing and cooing; this I mean very literally, for they would caress each other with their bills, and at the same time coo – the most unearthly coughings and cooings it is possible to imagine.

However, when once the egg was laid they carried on their flirtations underground. Rarely would the birds leave the egg alone, exposed to the risks of a visit from unwelcome rabbits or other birds. In turns they incubated it, one bird staying at the nest for from two to five days at a stretch, and as far as we could discover, the sitting bird did not leave the nest at all on these occasions, nor was it fed by its mate at night during these long spells of incubation. They were very tenacious and anxious about their one egg, and would peck our hands fiercely when we came once each day to examine the egg.

To enable us to make this study we had marked several burrows and cut a sod of earth out of the ground just above each nest, so that, at any time, by lifting up this sod, we could study the progress of the egg, and later of the chick.

We expected the egg to hatch at any time after four weeks had passed, but it was not until after the seventh week that signs of hatching were observed. In one case the chick had only just emerged on the 52nd day. In another nest we could hear the chick cheeping in the egg on the 52nd day, but this bird did not emerge until the 54th day.

The parents brooded the nestling in each case for one week, day and night, but afterwards they only came to feed it at night, when both parents would hold long conversations with the nestling in the recess. It was amusing to hear the absurd cooing of the parents and the faint, occasional 'Peep-peep-peep', very querulous and low, of the downy chick.

Of all the downy chicks of the bird world it would be difficult to find one more like a powder puff than the baby shearwater at six weeks old. It grows two lots of down, the first remaining attached to the second, so that, at six weeks, it is an immense ball of slate-grey down from which only the long beak protrudes. The bright, beady, black eyes are almost hidden by the down of the head.

Shortly after sprouting its feathers the young bird is entirely deserted by its one-time loving parents. By placing a sod at the mouth of the burrow we were able to note, by its position, whether a bird had entered or left the burrow, and thus to discover how long the nestling remained unfed in the nest. In each case it was about the sixtieth day that the young one, still very downy and not fully feathered, was completely deserted.

Six days later the young bird bestirred itself from the nest and made its first journey to the mouth of the burrow, pushing aside the sod, and leaving a trail of down at the burrow mouth to give evidence of its activity. It did not venture farther than the mouth of the burrow, but stayed there almost immovable during the midnight hours, a seemingly tragic figure. We felt compassion for the lonely little fellow, now seven days deserted and hungry. Wherever we walked on the island at night in early September these hungry, lonely little figures could be seen sitting patiently at the mouths of the burrows, waiting for the parents that would never come again. Before dawn they would return to their nests.

For six nights all told did our two specially marked birds keep vigil in the open and return to the burrow before dawn.

Then after those twelve days of fast they at last made off to the sea, and we did not see them again.

This journey from the nest to the sea is one of the most perilous adventures of these youngsters' lives. They are lucky if they have a high wind blowing when they first make up their minds to start, for a strong wind will often enable them to fly all the way from nest to sea, by giving them the necessary 'lift' upwards when they beat their wings in trying to rise off the ground.

The newly fledged shearwater is very unsteady on its legs and cannot make short runs on its toes as the adults can. If there is no wind it patters along the ground somehow, sustaining itself by beating its wings in the air, a most exhausting process which compels it to rest often. On uneven ground it pushes along with wings and legs, using its beak as well to surmount high objects. It is strange to see, in the dusk of night, these young birds making impulsive flutterings and scramblings, and anon resting awhile, towards the sea. They have great need to reach the sea the same night upon which they start from their nest. Should they be unable to do this, but instead find themselves still on land when dawn comes, their chances of remaining alive until the next evening are rather slender.

Almost before it is light the great black-backed gulls are beating over the fields and burrows and searching for these helpless young birds. The light of day seems to render the birds even more helpless and incapable of resistance. Lesser black-backed gulls, herring gulls, crows and buzzards also eagerly kill and devour the stranded young shearwaters, butchering them in a variety of styles peculiar to each bird of prey. On calm nights even the adult shearwaters are sometimes unable to rise from heather and bracken, when they too are caught in the open upon the following day and killed. The toll is heavy. In one season I could reckon the remains of over fifteen hundred birds on the island cliffs and meadows.

At night the young birds tumble straight over the cliffs when they reach them, and flutter down into the sea. Here, at last, they are in their own element, a limitless place where food and drink can be found. One bird we carried to the sea first alleviated its thirst by daintily drinking and then proceeded to wash itself very thoroughly. All the young birds are expert swimmers and divers, using their wings to swim under water. One imagines that they have little difficulty in quickly obtaining a meal of sprats or fry and thus breaking their long fast.

FIFTEEN

Winter

S UMMERS HAVE THEIR ENDINGS, and winters perforce must come with all its wild storms and rough seas. We had many winter adventures; not all of them I should care to experience again, but this one was pleasant enough.

Doris, I and John had left the island on Friday with a gale from the southwest threatening us. The breeze that blew us across to the mainland was already so fresh that the infant motor was unnecessary and the lug had to be reefed.

The gale came on in the afternoon, and blew until Sunday at midnight, when it abated, so we prepared to return at dawn on Monday morning. The breeze was now west and still so fresh that John, deeming it impossible for us to get down to the island, remained in the village, intending to come down to the Haven at the proper time of tide for the passage to the island.

The red sky of morning threatened a day of bad weather and, as the one responsible for the ferrying of the rabbit catch from the island, I was anxious to go across and bring it back to the mainland, and then return to the island. 'In coarse weather,' a fisherman had warned us, 'it is not safe to travel up and down these Sounds with a crew of one novice and his wife.' Two trained men were needed, both able, if required, to pull a fourteen-foot oar for hours at a time.

But Doris and I, as soon as the wind began to fall to a gentle sailing breeze, were seized with sea fever again, and we put to sea alone, intending to cruise about St Bride's Bay until it was time to take the current for our island. I am not ashamed to say that I love our boat, and whenever there's a pleasant sailing breeze my desire is to be sailing her. I love best a beam wind, for then the boat sails with tight sheets, heels over a little and cuts bravely through the water. There was an extra exhilaration today, because we had not been able to sail about alone for several days; moreover, the Skomer boat had just left the Haven to return to Skomer, and as we pushed our boat down the pebbles to launch her was even then creeping sluggishly towards Skomer, soullessly hugging the rocks so as to keep out of the wind. There were five people aboard this Skomer boat, and all five could appreciate the sight of our rigged boat beating against a headwind.

There was too much headwind to beat without the help of the 'Infant,' so we started her bawling as soon as we pushed off, and I began, with sailorly pleasure, to hoist sail. First, I stepped our tall white mast, then I ran up the white lug mainsail. Doris headed her after the Skomer boat, which was nearly at Skomer by now, while I ran up the jib.

A bowsprit is a serious inconvenience when we are launching or landing our boat in the narrow gut of the boatslip on the island, and in consequence we make an oar serve, by tying it to one thwart and to the ring in the stem of the boat, so that some three feet of the handle end protrudes from the bow in the true fashion of all self-respecting bowsprits. To the extreme end of the oar the jib is tied. On this occasion I ran up the jib, and made all fast. The *Storm Petrel* caught the west wind on her port beam, heeled over and, with the Infant helping, shaped a course for Skomer North Haven, heading northwest by west on this first tack. I hope and believe the poor men of

Skomer, rowing their tub-like craft like galley slaves, saw the white sides of the *Storm Petrel* as she lay over to the breeze, saw her red gunwale line making a margin below her white mainsail, her white flying jib upon the bowsprit, and enjoyed the rare sight. Such is the conceit of boat owners!

As Doris had never been in the North Haven of Skomer, it was our intention to tack swiftly into this little harbour upon the stern of the Skomer boat. Doris would then have had the opportunity of admiring that lovely haven, and if our good friends the residents invited us ashore – well, all such little adventures are welcome. There is freedom and adventure in sailing one's own boat to foreign shores.

When we had stood out long enough on this first tack, long enough for us to see that the Skomer boat had landed and was being hauled up the little beach there, we came about and headed southwest on the second tack, making for the Rye Rocks of North Haven. The Little Sound lay invitingly before us, with our own island far below. How easy it seemed to go on down to our home with this pleasant breeze to help defeat the tide that must perforce be all against us.

It was high time we learned the tricks of the sea in winter. We could not be forever dependent on fishermen.

The temptation was too much for us. The sky was half-filled with heavy rainclouds to the south; the north was full of blue, rapidly diminishing as the clouds came out of the west. The current was already making up through the Little Sound against us. Nevertheless, the *Storm Petrel* urged us to be sailing across the open seas for home, and we abandoned ourselves to her mood, forgetting our cruise to Skomer North Haven; forgetting the astonished men of Skomer, whose traditions of tide we might be destroying; only glad to be sailing in full canvas for the shores of our distant island.

The Infant cried joyously to be battling a tide again. We let the boat point due south through the Little Sound, slackening the sheets to take a fairer wind. There was a short tussle with the tide where it ran strongest in the Little Sound, but the *Storm Petrel* emerged triumphant and sailed away across the sea for our island.

The rest was easy. It suited the boat to be dragged out westwards a little by the tide, as this enabled us to sail with a fairer breeze. We reached the Stack, the nearest point of the island, in thirty minutes and easily defeated the northwest-going current there. A few minutes later we were in our own harbour, South Haven, as pleased as two mortals could be, and a quarter of an hour later we had loaded our cargo and the Infant was taking us out of the harbour on our voyage back to the mainland.

The wind had now dwindled to the faintest breeze, which barely filled our mainsail, and out of which it was continuously being spilt by the lumpiness of the ground sea, which caused the boat to roll and bump. But the clouds in the west had been quietly gathering and now a heavy squall of rain hung over us, threatening to deluge us at any moment. Though the sail hung almost idly, and I was helping the Infant with one oar, I had a not quite comfortable feeling that presently the mainsail would be more than enough to drive us to the Haven on the mainland. And so it proved.

A sailing breeze sprang up as the rain began to fall, and in a few moments it freshened as the rain became heavier. Before I could comfortably make up my mind to reef the mainsail (the jib, of course, was not out), rain and wind became violent and we were driven furiously into Jack Sound, the sea suddenly becoming alive with white horses. The Infant was of no use at all, and roared louder and louder as the wind carried the boat at a break mast speed. A rabbit-catcher working on the cliffs above Jack Sound described to me later that our pace had been 'marvellous,' an adjective calculated to please a boat-lover.

We turned the corner into the Haven with no little relief. The sail flapped under the shelter of the rocky shore. The Infant ceased its useless roar and settled down quietly to the business of bringing us to the Haven's pebble beach.

This was our first winter passage alone, and gave us confidence for the many that followed.

There are some people in the world who have no sense of fear; Doris is one of them. For my part I have to admit to little fears and flutterings at moments of necessary decision or crisis. Doris is perpetually prepared to go out to sea in the face of any reasonable gale. It is hard for me to say her nay when she expects to put forth in a mild hurricane. It is, besides, damaging to one's self-esteem to have to admit that it cannot be done, no matter how prudent the decision may be. If we do not fare forth and the wind falls a little, one is a little disgusted with oneself. If a gale really does blow, all one feels is a little smug satisfaction, the merest ghost of a feeling.

It is hard, therefore, to decide what to do when the wind is only half a gale and half a breeze. Can one put to sea? Wisdom says no, youth and action dictate yes. Presently, I feel sure, experience will tell us how unwise it is to set out in bad weather. For the day on which the following adventure befell proved to be one of bad weather indeed, and I have no wish to repeat the experience.

The blame, if any, must partly be laid upon Richard, my rabbit-catcher, of whom more anon.

One bright morning, in October, after a day or two of rough weather, Doris and I left the island in charge of John, as we now often did, and sailed to Martynshaven. I say sailed, but it was only a pretence of sailing. What little breeze there was about was rendered useless by the ground swell, which upset it from out the sails. Still it is, next to actual sailing, a fine thing to pretend to sail – to have all the canvas out in full glory with sheets tight to prevent undue flapping. On this occasion the Infant was moving all the while along with the tide, and I helping with a lazy oar.

We got to the Haven, disgorged our cargo, and hauled the boat above the tide with the handwinch. Richard had promised to meet us, and come back to work on the island. But he failed to appear, and after waiting for several hours, during which we were busier about other things than merely waiting for a procrastinating rabbit-catcher, I went over on my bicycle to hunt him down in his native village.

Tracking a man of moods, such as Richard is, is no easy task, and on this occasion it meant the visiting of several cottages, where I was given all the local gossip as to Richard's past, present and future movements. It chiefly appeared that Richard had been playing an auctioneering game with the lords of the islands, with Me (of the Lower Island), and with Him of Skomer. He had been trying to sell himself for a higher wage to Skomer, well knowing that he might then compel me, possibly, to pay more than his usual wage, which, as a matter of fact, was above the standard rate.

Richard is an old man, yet clever at his profession, and one has perforce to take his peculiarities as they come. I could write many pages about him, but not now, for I have not yet come to the adventure of which I would speak. Let me finish with Richard for the present by adding that I found him in his cottage garden, and being already armed with the knowledge that he would get no more wages on Skomer, I threatened him with a mild ultimatum that his last chance this winter would be tomorrow, when he must finally decide to be, or not to be, ready on the beach at sunrise. For it was now dusk and too late to think of crossing that night. Richard promised, faithfully again, to turn up in the morning.

The sunrise next day was lurid and stormy, and with a faint heart I looked out upon the sea, which was running high by reason of a strong west wind. It was not fit weather to cross. Richard would not face it, I knew, and he did not even put in an appearance. To consult Doris under the circumstances seemed the only thing to do, so I laid the case before her.

'We can get down to the Lower Island if we go at once, and provided the Infant keeps her song true and steady. Also, I think there's a possibility of sailing if the wind goes up a little.' Doris was fearless in the matter, but experience had taught her by now to leave our fate in my hands for decision.

Now it is difficult to say no when your wife looks so ready and courageous enough to tackle anything with you. I had not therefore the heart to say no while there was half a chance. But with the wind as it was, strong and westerly, today I had only half a heart to go and half to stay. The casting vote was given by Doris, who merely said that she was longing to get home. So we set forth.

Lustily roared the Infant, as if knowing what need we had of her, and I pulled a hearty oar, while Doris took the tiller. The sea was a smother of white at Tusker Rock, but we safely crossed Jack Sound and pointed her to windward. We could not make our 'westing' enough to put up sail, and I

was sorry we had not gone through the Little Sound instead of Jack Sound.
I soon saw, too, that we were going to have our work cut out to reach the
island at all, for the tide and wind were both going east. The Infant did its
best; I did mine with an oar, and, if looks could have helped, Doris, who
was thoroughly enjoying it, including the salt spray, would have got us
home in good time.

Suddenly, without any warning to me – for I sat rowing, back to the bow
– a green sea came inboard, effectually silencing the Infant as it washed
down past the engine into the bilge trap. There was nothing now to be
done save to bail this green fellow out as quickly as possible, and this
I set out to do at once, while Doris kept the boat's head on to the seas
with the paddles. The wind had been freshening all the time, and drove us
eastwards while the tide dragged us south.

Bailing completed, I tried to persuade the wet and discomforted Infant
to recommence work. She did her best but, after a few apologetic coughs,
was unable to oblige us. Clearly she wanted a good cleaning and drying.
Meanwhile our beloved island home drifted to windward and we to
leeward. We saw our harbour come into view, looking green and sweet,
but far away to windward and unget-at-able. The sea gathered strength
from the wind every moment.

One chance now was left to us: to put up sail and run for it before
the wind to Milford Haven, braving the tumultuous seas and striving tide
races outside St Ann's head.

Fairly caught in the gale now, the *Storm Petrel* tossed, dipped and
curvetted as she was borne towards St Ann's by the wind-roughened tide.
I reefed the lug mainsail, stepped our tall, white mast with a little effort
owing to the tossing of the boat, and ran up the canvas. Instantly the boat
gave up her sluggish drifting and leaped forward. I made one last effort
before I let her run away. The sheet was close-hauled, and the *Storm Petrel*
headed for the island while I again tackled the engine. But all things were
against us. The sheet flapped in the headwind and we began to go astern;
the tide carried us away and the Infant failed to bawl. So we turned around
and let her go for Milford Haven and the high, white-crested rollers that

pounded on the great cliffs of St Ann's head.

The *Storm Petrel* is a grand boat, and well built to stand work on the open sea. As she flew away before the gale, she rode the seas easily, barely shipping as much as a gallon of water. Sometimes the big rollers curled over and crashed behind and before us, but she moved faster than these breakers and slipped away from beneath them. Now her bow would be six feet clear, standing in the air on the crest of a wave, and then she would plunge down the slope and her nose would be level with the water, which would look over the gunwale as if it would enter and swamp us; but our brave boat would rise eagerly, shaking the water from her dripping freeboard and resume the race again.

After a little while, and after some very formidable breakers had been negotiated without serious distress to the boat, I began to take pleasure in the experience. I was assured by her behaviour that the *Storm Petrel* would weather all the seas in front as easily as she had done those behind. As for Doris, that fearless lady had enjoyed every anxious second, I believe. She was completely happy when we both sat in the stern thwart and settled down together on this wild cruise for shelter.

We afterwards found that John and Henry had watched our whole performance from the island, and the men at the island lighthouse had been standing by to send up signals as soon as an extra big wave engulfed us. This was very courteous of the latter, though when we passed St Ann's Head the coastguards there did not appear to have seen us at all, even when we were in the midst of the tide races of the south stream from the Channel, and the ebb tide of Milford Haven, which, at this point, and at certain hours of every day, strive together in motley confusion.

However, there was no need for undue anxiety. The *Storm Petrel* passed through the inferno at St Ann's Head without taking much water inboard, and sailed on up Milford Haven to the quiet waters of the bays and inlets there. Dale Roads was full of ships taking shelter in that anchorage, and two trawlers, going out to sea from Milford Dock, turned back on encountering the swell from St Ann's and made for the same place. Even in these Roads the west wind made a choppy sea, and I preferred to sail on to Sandy Haven, where we could obtain perfect security, quietness and hospitality for the night.

The tide was at low water so we had to wait our chance to sail up the creek of Sandy Haven. We eventually ran ashore on some pebbles east of Great Castle Head, had a meal, basked for a little in the sun, and when the tide was nearing full flood continued up the creek. I had dealt firmly with the Infant meanwhile, and she sang bravely again, landing us in proper fashion beside Sandy Haven quay.

The owner of this quay, Captain Cristal, who had assisted us to dismantle the *Alice Williams*, extended a hearty welcome, and made us free of his house, while his amiable wife prepared us that warm meal which hungry *voyageurs* are so capable of appreciating.

There is a magic stillness in the air of Sandy Haven, and we slept soundly in that windless place where nothing can ever happen; where gales are not heard; where the water is perpetually smooth, and where a man may lay down to sleep without fear for his ship's safety.

We were duly acquainted with the history and local gossip of the neighbourhood from our good hostess, and learnt, among other things, that a kitten might be had for the asking at a place up the creek on the opposite shore. Our cruise was, therefore, not to be a fruitless run and only for shelter. From that moment it was apparent that our whole object had been to obtain a kitten from some place inside Milford Haven.

While the tide was still making that night we went across in the *Storm Petrel* and were given a pretty white- and tabby-marked kitten. He was promptly stowed on board, made cabin boy and named 'Mousse.'

The next morning was cold and rainy, and with faint hope in our hearts we sailed away at dawn, going down to Dale on an easterly breeze. A mighty swell came rolling in from the Atlantic, and it was clearly blowing hard outside St Ann's. We therefore put about and motored back to Sandy Haven, running aground just before the tide ebbed too far to allow of our getting up the creek. We then left the *Storm Petrel* there on the mud and explored the bylanes of this foreign country, the rain having now been blown away by a wind from east-northeast.

When the tide came in, late in the afternoon, we said goodbye to our host and hostess, with many thanks for harbourage of boat and man, and, not forgetting Mousse, set sail with better heart for the open sea. There was still a heavy swell, but the sea was unbroken and the breeze fair all the way home. The only difficulty now would be in landing in the surf of the swell. I prayed that my good John and Henry would be standing by to haul the boat up as soon as she touched our crazy slipway.

Two coastguards looked at us curiously as we passed under the cliffs of St Ann's, the *Storm Petrel* in full sail, mainsail and jib-upon-bowsprit, riding the angry swell with untroubled serenity. Tide and wind were in our favour, and we made a glorious passage over the sunset-coloured sea. The sun dropped behind the island as we approached, but we could see our little harbour white with the dancing temper of the ground sea, last legacy of the storm.

The only thing to do was to make a painter ready on her bow, run in upon the slip with the Infant's help, trust that the gods would restrain the wash of the sea for the space of time required to make the boat fast to the cable and so haul her clear of the angry swell. It was a ticklish business. Three hands held to the painter, and as the swells came rushing in and lifted the stern of the boat, all three hauled mightily; the fourth man lustily wound the slack wire tight on the winch, till presently the cable tautened and the good ship shook the water off her to ride gently up the rough slip and to come to rest in her steep berth.

What delight there is in an island home when one lands and makes safe the boat after a voyage: more especially after a perilous one! The rafters of our cottage gleamed warmly in the firelight that night, and Mousse lay at his ease in the warmth of the timber fire on our wide, welcoming hearth.

SIXTEEN
Gales

THERE ARE CERTAIN LIMITS to safe boating on the open sea, and the more often one touches those limits the more careful one becomes to avoid them. In other words, experience teaches us caution, and, in John's favourite words, 'It's better to make sure than to be sorry.' I shall never again moor my boat off in the haven overnight – in winter.

It happened that the morning was calm one winter's day, when we went across to the mainland; and when we were ready to return to the island again a northerly breeze sprang up to help us. We sailed home swiftly before the wind, arriving back barely three hours after having left in the morning, and with all our mainland business done for the week.

When the wind is in the north, the south-facing South Haven of our island is as tranquil as the traditional millpond. The fiercest northerly gale cannot make rough the sheltered water below the high walls of the landing place. Therefore we often sigh for northerly breezes, but get them rarely in winter, at least, no longer than for a casual day at a time.

So quiet and smooth was South Haven that day that I decided we would leave the boat at her moorings. At that time we had a cork buoy marking the mooring chain and anchor. An endless rope ran from a block on this chain to the ring bolt on the cliff and back again. The method was to bend the boat's painter on to this rope; the boat could then be run from the cliff to the buoy on the endless rope after landing, and vice versa when we wished to embark. But this type of mooring was exposed to the water all the time; the ropes soon rotted, and, as we found subsequently, the first big southerly gale swept everything completely away. The moorings, however, had stood during and since the summer until the day of which I speak.

Dusk soon comes down on November days, and on this occasion the wind died away until there was but a faint breeze from the north. John and I looked down from the landing at the moored *Storm Petrel* lying listlessly on the calm water. Surely it was safe to leave her for one night thus, while the breeze was in the north? How many times had we left her moored in the summer? We remembered that there had been a period of days so calm that the boat had never once been berthed on the island slip for a whole month. Perhaps we were in for another calm spell. We agreed there could be no harm in leaving her for this one night, so we saluted her in the dusk and bade her goodnight. There she lay, with all her gear neatly stowed along the thwarts: her sails, her mast and her oars. We left her sleeping on the water, and we ourselves went to bed later, confident that all was well, tired with the day's work and ready to sleep.

It was five in the morning when I woke to hear the loud moan above my head. For a moment I listened, trying to make out the direction of the wind, expecting that the northerly breeze had freshened. In that case, of course, all would still be well. But the wind seemed to be pressing and moaning on the slates on the south roof of the house. Moreover, the east-facing bedroom window was whistling as the wind pressed upon it. I knew then that it was the dreaded southeast wind that was freshening – the hostile wind that so quickly blows into South Haven and raises mountainous seas there.

John, Richard and Henry were sleeping in a rehabilitated cottage next to the Wheelhouse. I expected the watchful John would already have heard the wind and thought of the boat, and when I ran out to the cottage I found him stirring up his companions. In the darkness we all felt our way down to South Haven. At every moment the wind was increasing, and with it my anxiety.

I think my heart missed several beats when I first peered down into the white foam of the sea in South Haven and saw no dark shape of my boat dancing on the water. How much I valued and cared for the *Storm Petrel* I realised then. It seemed to me that I was facing the greatest disaster in my life, for a swift fleeting memory of all the sunny voyages she had given us came to me.

In the darkness before the late dawn, however, I had been deceived, for when we all got down near the landing steps we could see the precious boat afloat and straining at her moorings as she rode up and down over the foaming waves which the wind drove in past her. Great was our relief!

To get at her was a different matter. It was not yet high water, but the waves splashed so high on the cliff where the mooring rope was fastened that neither John nor I could get down to unfasten it. Even had we been able to do so, it would still have been impossible in the darkness to get down over the wave-beaten rocks and jump aboard. We were compelled to wait for daylight.

The wind, now steadily rising to gale force, roared up the ravine of the haven and was bitterly cold. We were therefore glad to drink the hot tea Doris brought us. It warmed us a little as we crouched against the cliff, our eyes watching, between the showers of salt spray, for the moorings to part and let the *Storm Petrel* be smashed on the rocks below us.

Dawn and high water came together. We could barely see the ropes now, for the heavy seas were constantly over them. But still the *Storm Petrel* rode the smother, head-on to wind and breakers. Each time she slanted up the wave, and then headlong down it, my heart plunged with her. I expected her every moment to bury her nose into the slant of the next close-rising wave, but she never quite plunged under. The most anxious moments were those when she slewed round a little, edging broadside-on in the trough of the waves. How the sea shook her then! Furiously to and fro it tossed and rocked her, making her now wallow in the trough and now pitch lengthwise on the breaking top. When half-broadside on she shipped water heavily, and it was with great relief that I saw her move to a head-on position again.

But this could not go on. More and more water was splashing inboard until she was half full. Her movements gradually grew heavy and sluggish; she did not ride so well, but plunged sullenly, taking every curl of foam and wave crest inboard. We saw – I almost in despair – her stern sheets and loose wooden parts floating about inside her and the engine quite under water.

To swim out to her would be madness; the waves would overwhelm one if the first plunge did not end in striking the rocks. It seemed we must watch her sink at her moorings; and, certainly, any boat less seaworthy than the broad-beamed *Storm Petrel* would have done so.

When at last there was perceptible evidence of the ebb, and we could see the rope more often, John and I climbed down to the ring bolt. As we unfastened the rope wave after wave dashed upon us, and as each one came we held desperately on to the cliff face.

John was the hero of this episode. Well-used to rock-climbing, at which pursuit he reminds me of a fly upon a perpendicular wall, he stood waiting for the chance to make a flying leap into the boat. I manoeuvred the ropes, gradually pulling the boat, as near as I dared, into the cliff. Then, when there seemed to be at last a small interval between the pounding waves I yelled 'Ready!' and pulled the boat in hard. John, standing twenty feet above the water, ran headlong down over the sharp, steep cliff and made a brave and spectacular leap into the boat. Instantly, I pulled on the reverse rope and gradually worked the boat out into the middle of the haven, away from the treacherous rocks.

John's weight, plus the water she had taken aboard, nearly sank the *Storm Petrel*. As it was I had to warn him not to stand anywhere except amidships. I could see the water pouring in through the engine exhaust outlets, as the gunwale came level with the water. The oars and gear were about to float away. I shouted warnings, but am doubtful if he heard them in the noise of wind and wave.

He was expending all his energies upon bailing.

The small bailing scoop seemed ridiculously inadequate to remove hundreds of gallons of water, and for many minutes it seemed that he could not gain upon the amount of water still being dashed in. Up and down he was tossed with the boat as she rode heavily on the waves. I could feel the heavy strain of her weight on the mooring-rope when I touched it with my hands. At any moment it must go. It was badly chafed in several places by the rocks already.

And just as John had gained on the water in the boat with his scoop the mooring-rope chafed right through.

John was now satisfied that he could bail her out, and began to scoop out with less frenzied movements. When he saw that the rope had parted he tied the broken ends to the boat in order to stop them running out of the block on the mooring chain and continued to finish his job. Then he cast off the ropes, swung a paddle in the stern and sculled into the comparative shelter of the slipway. Even here, however, there were breaking waves, and it needed both of us to hold the *Storm Petrel* on the slip until the cable on the winch, operated by Richard and Henry, at last dragged the boat to safety.

Never again have I moored the boat overnight in winter.

November and December are the months of the greatest storms and rains here. January is quieter; February generally cold with dry, easterly winds. Thereafter, March, April and May are often the quietest months of the year. During three winters the worst gales we have experienced have come in November.

It was in mid-November that a terrific hurricane struck the island. For a whole week there had been southwesterly gales, until, on the fifteenth of the month, they abated and left only light airs from the west.

In spite of this lightness of wind, however, there was a very heavy ground sea rolling in from the Atlantic. By dashing upon the cliffs of Mad Bay, and about the lighthouse, this sent as much spray over the island as if a gale were actually blowing.

The crossing John and I made that day was not entirely to my liking. I felt a bit doubtful of the immense ground seas which rolled majestically through the Broad Sound. Here and there, in spite of the lack of wind, where a rock or shoal rose within a dozen fathoms of the surface, the wave crests would break in long, white array. A boat would stand no chance if such a crest broke upon it, and, therefore, we kept well away from any shallow ground.

When we passed through Jack Sound we chose a middle course; we dare not pass near the cliffs, where the wash of the sea was terrific. Even the usually quiet waters of Martynshaven were agitated, and we had to choose the right moment between breaking waves at which to run aground.

A good imitation of a ground sea may be made by breathing or blowing hard upon the surface of a bowl or bath of water. The disturbed surface is at once marked by outward-moving ripples, which travel far and wide over the area before gradually diminishing in height and dying away until they are imperceptible. These ripples, which correspond to the swell of a ground sea caused by a blow of wind, dash against the sides of the bath just as the swell does against the cliffs. They indicate that somewhere the water has been disturbed by wind, and that a gale is, or has been, in the vicinity. When these swells gradually lessen in height and strength you may feel easier in mind that the storm has passed away from your neighbourhood.

Now on this occasion they continued so to increase, to roar louder and wilder on the coasts, that John and I hurried to return to the island before the approaching gale arrived. I was very glad when we at last got into South Haven, using the motor only; for there was less wind than ever in the afternoon. With so little wind it would have been impossible to sail, for the swells so rocked the boat that the sails would have done nothing but shake and flap. From the crest of one swell to the crest of the next is a distance of perhaps fifty yards, while the height, reckoned from the bottom of the troughs to the crests, is about fifteen feet; though it seems nearer thirty when one sinks down into the trough and can see nothing but the slopes of the swells on each side. These measurements of an Atlantic swell, when running before a gale, are of course only an approximate calculation.

The swells always come in from the ocean out westward. They strike on the extreme westerly points of Mad Bay and the Head, and roll along the north and south cliffs until they reunite eastwards of the island. Because of this, South Haven escapes the direct pounding of these swells, sheltered as it is by rocks and cliffs from the west. Excepting, therefore, when the southeast wind blows into the harbour we can usually launch the boat, for the strength of the swell has diminished by the time it reaches the boat slip. Nevertheless, there are some days when this roll is too high and rough to allow the boat to be handled, and when we got back that afternoon we had a very ticklish few minutes in hauling the *Storm Petrel* up the slip. It had been bad enough launching with a full cargo in the morning, but now, when we ran upon the slip, the sea left us dry at one moment and at the next floating atop of the sea that rushed in.

All that night we could hear the great thunder as of a thousand distant guns booming. It was the ground sea crashing on the cliffs, and the sound was very clear on the windless night air.

In the morning a gale from southeast was raging: a good, solid ordinary sou'easter with hurrying dark clouds. Then the sky suddenly cleared and the wind veered to southwest. But it began to blow in earnest just before noon, and reached its greatest force at noon. I have never felt, or seen, anything so furious and wild as that hurricane.

The shriek of the wind gradually rose to a high whistle, which shrilled in my ears to the exclusion of all other sounds. Although I was standing within a few feet of a two-foot-thick wall, which was blown down in front of my eyes, I heard not a sound of the crashing masonry. Some twelve feet of this wall, nine feet high, was blown out of one of the farm folds, and almost immediately afterwards a similar-sized section was blown out of a fold wall next to the Wheelhouse, carrying with it the corner stones of the Wheelhouse itself.

There are times when we think of the sea and the wind as sweet, clean and kind things; merciful to man and his possessions. But that is when there are calm days, or light summer breezes, and perhaps when the sea is warm and teeming with fish life. Yet, though we may love wind and sea, we learn to know that they are impersonal, incapable of pity for us; hard and cruel; as ready to destroy utterly, as to bestow generously, when we encounter them. That day sea and wind came tearing and shrieking at the island with intent to kill and destroy.

By no means satisfied with toppling over two high walls, the gale sought to lift off every roof. It screamed in the slates of the house until I grew anxious; but when building I had riveted the edge of every slate to its neighbour and not a slate moved on the main roof. But in spite of its solid walls, in places three feet thick, the house quivered with the strength of the gale, and the roar all about the outside walls was terrific.

The roofs of the Wheelhouse and of the house porch are tiled with island stone, and soon there were many gaps, for the heavy tiles came flying off at several points. The corrugated iron roof of the cottage and store rooms we just managed to save by piling immense stones, as much as three of us could lift together, upon it.

The house and all the buildings enjoy some shelter from the southwest by the configuration of the land in that direction. We wondered what it must be like at the lighthouse, which stood shelterless directly in the path of the gale. Later we learned that the sea had been battering to the top of the cliff, one hundred feet high, the spindrift running into the yards and down the mouth of the foghorn at the top of the building. The heavy wooden fence round the gardens, which lie sheltered behind an outcrop of rock, was destroyed, and the vegetables withered up. So, too, were our own green things. Everything was covered with a thick crust of salt, even in our sheltered gardens.

The long grass of the bog was torn up bodily and blown in drifts into the yards and folds, while most of it was carried away entirely, rising higher and higher into the blue sky.

While this gale was at its height the sky was clear, excepting for an occasional, racing, white wisp of cloud, but as night came on, and the wind abated considerably, heavy clouds came up. We hauled the boat up to the very wheel of the winch. At low water South Haven was a sad sight, presenting to us a mass of jagged, ugly rocks instead of a smooth beach for landing on. The sea had washed all the pebbles out below low watermark, and we knew it would be months before they would be gradually washed back again.

For more than a week afterwards the sea continued to leap twenty feet above the topmost point of the Stack, and there was no venturing out upon it.

One winter's day, after crossing to the mainland for stores and letters, I was cut off from the island by a freshening wind. This increased to a great hurricane and all thoughts of returning to Skokholm that day were abandoned.

Towards dusk only an ordinary gale was blowing. The sun had set behind racing clouds when I went out along the headland to bid goodnight to my island. I wondered how soon the sea would go down to the measure of stillness required for a crossing to my home. Far out to sea in the southwest the red light of the island lighthouse winked me a reply. Westwards across Jack Sound lay the little island of Midland and beyond it the dark mass of Skomer and her gigantic Mewstone Rock.

Then, quite suddenly, I saw the bow and foremast of a ship silhouetted as it protruded from the black background of Midland. Sharply and clearly her bow stood out, her very keel showing beneath her forefoot. Then a monstrous billow rolled in and overwhelmed her. The end of things, I thought, filled with horror. But no! The great wave subsided, ebbed until the ship stood gaunt and naked as before, then, gathering strength, heaved up and buried her again. At the height of the gale, which had raged all day, she had been thrown on the rocks. Now the sea pounded her, and played with her as a cat with a mouse, before swallowing her completely. There was no light shining as a sign of life aboard, and no sound could reach across Jack Sound. The wind in my ears was such that I could barely hear the thunder of the surf two hundred feet below me.

I did not know then that thirty people were huddled amidships in a tiny cabin, shuddering at each of the ocean's blows. Nothing, I thought, could live, surely, in that terrible sea!

Hardly had I left the headland than in the lane by my hut I met the first coastguard (arrived by car from the wireless station at Fishguard), who reported that the SS *Molesey* had wirelessed 'gone ashore on Wooltack Point.' That was the last message sent by her.

'A total loss; she'll never live in this sea!' he said.

He took down my depositions as to the position of the wreck on the southeast shore of Midland. She was certainly not on Wooltack Point, the headland on which we were standing, but immediately opposite us and quite out of reach half a mile across Jack Sound. No doubt her captain had confused the headlands in sending his message.

Hurrying back into the lane on our way to the village we met the male population coming solidly towards us in the dark, seated on or running behind a lorry loaded with the breeches buoy and life-saving rocket apparatus from St Ann's Head. Of no avail: no rocket could span Jack Sound; and as soon as the hopeless position of the wreck was known the lorry was turned back. Already the two local motor lifeboats, keen rivals, had, according to report, left their stations at Angle and St Davids, and were out searching.

The Marloes men must also help. As the only man to have seen the wreck properly, it was for me to organise a crew. Twenty men answered my appeal as one man. I called out the first five who showed their hands.

Nothing could be done that night in the howling wind. The rendezvous was Martynshaven at dawn, where we would launch our biggest boat. But long before dawn we were out upon the headland, sleep far from us, our hearts longing for the wind to abate. We watched the white run of the tide anxiously.

It must have been at low water that at last a sign of life came from the darkness where we knew the ship was lying. One or two rockets shot up, their blue light revealing an iron deck swept as bare as the palm of my hand. Encouraged by this unexpected glimpse, with new hope in our hearts, we ran down to the dark cove where the boats lay. Just as our scratch crew was launching, the headlights of a car drew down upon the beach. The principals of the firm owning the *Molesey* hastened to tell us that there were some thirty souls comprising the crew of the wrecked ship.

The sky in the east was growing pale when we set out, unwillingly pushing back half-a-dozen volunteers who would have overloaded us. The six of us rowed and rowed, for my part as never before, with those long sea-sweeps. Half a mile of such pulling brought us to that rocky cauldron of wind-roughened currents which is Jack Sound.

It was now light enough for us to see the *Molesey* lying tilted against Midland, her smoke-stack flat as cardboard, her bridge and upper works carried right away. We saw, however, that there was life on board, and we pulled harder than ever.

Slowly foot by foot with tide and oars we crossed Jack Sound against the fierce west wind.

We were fewer than one hundred yards from the wreck, toiling painfully but surely along, tossed and battered by the swell, when the Angle lifeboat, new, full-powered with twin engines, came grandly up from southwards at top speed, crashing through the waves as she swept in front of us. Throwing out anchors, she backed upon them until she had drawn alongside the wreck. One by one the survivors threw themselves down upon her. There were more than eight missing, reported swept overboard in the night.

Pleased that all were saved, yet, I must confess, disappointed to have had no share in their rescue, we drifted back upon the island of Midland. With some difficulty we put ashore a landing party to see if any survivors had reached the island in the night. There was none. A few minutes later the wind had blown us back to Martynshaven.

I was anxious now to return to my island, but it was much too rough to cross that day. Even on the following morning it was none too pleasant when John and I set out. Our course lay past the *Molesey*. We were tempted to board her and explore. Something of John's fever to loot and pillage a wreck has by now crept into my veins. We reduced speed as we passed her. All doubts as to whether we had better stop, in view of the sightseers now rapidly crowding on to the headland opposite, were dispelled when we heard a feeble call from near the ship.

One last survivor, a Maltese fireman, yesterday hidden, semiconscious, in a berth during the lifeboat rescue, and now supposing all others drowned but himself, was signalling desperately to us. He had jumped into the sea with nothing but a lifebelt and vest on, and was now standing on the rocks below the ship. Almost before we were alongside he fell into the *Storm Petrel*, over-eagerly, bruising his battered body, which was half-frozen and trembling with fright and exposure.

We could get no sense out of him, so I left him with John, and while he was being fed out of our stores, wrapped warmly and given the thing he craved most – tobacco – I scrambled aboard the wreck to look for other survivors. In vain; I saw only devastation – and a possible opportunity to collect some useful 'wreck.'

We sped back with Pola Attard to Martynshaven, left him in good hands there, and then sailed home once more, to hear Doris's account of the wreck and the rescue, as seen from our island.

We never got a chance, unfortunately, to raid the *Molesey*, as we did to our hearts' content the *Alice Williams*. Afterwards we learned that no one was allowed to remove or salvage a single item during the two calm days that followed. All her beautiful furniture, her tools and fittings were senselessly sacrificed by the underwriters to the gale that soon came and swept her to the bottom. Her furniture and wooden parts, battered to uselessness, floated away to distant beaches, and were picked up for firewood. I regretted especially a nice lathe I saw on her.

Now, at dead low water of spring tides, only the iron heart of her lies visible, given over to the fishes and the long ribbony seaweeds.

SEVENTEEN

The year turns

So far february has each year been a month when easterly winds have prevailed; the coldest month of the year. We do not mind these cold winds, which blow from off the land, as they bring us calm seas and dry weather after the winter storms. Not often does it rain from the east, and rarely are there flurries of snow. The only snow we have had in three winters came in February 1929 – our second winter – but it came then all at once and in earnest.

In the middle of the month frosts set in. As a rule frost rarely visits the island with any severity, but now, for four days, there were intense frosts, which held the ground very hard. At the same time there were extremely bitter winds from east and southeast. So strong were these that they caused rough water even on the ponds, and thus prevented their freezing over.

With the intense cold came great flocks of westward-flying birds. An east wind always brings us more visitors in the winter, and now, day after day, hundreds of starlings, thrushes, redwings, fieldfares, lapwing and golden plover arrived; snipe and jack snipe, too; woodcock, curlew, blackbirds, meadow pipits, larks, wrens, robins, linnets, chaffinches and greenfinches in small flocks. On the edges of the two ponds wigeon, mallard and teal congregated, and once or twice small skeins of wild geese joined them.

Many of these visitors did not stop long, but hurried on westwards into the limitless Atlantic, some heading in a direction that would eventually land them in America, if they did and could continue so far; others made towards Grassholm, and in a northerly direction towards Ireland. The larks, pipits and starlings usually flew very low over the waves; the lapwing, curlew and golden plover flying very high in the air, often so high as barely to be seen and recognised.

Indeed, on a previous occasion – December 17th, 1927 – I saw immense flocks of lapwing crossing at considerable height in a due west direction, flying at tremendous speed before a southeasterly gale. A few days later many lapwing were noticed on the east coast of Canada, where they perished in the cold and snow; and I often think that these may have been some of the very birds that flew over the island so precipitately before the bitter gale, and, failing to touch Ireland at all, may have continued onwards on a two-thousand-mile flight to Newfoundland, where most of these birds were first seen.

The frozen state of the ground made it a difficult matter for the great numbers of birds to find food, and the strong, penetrating winds added to their misery. Starlings dug at the hard ground unavailingly, and had to turn their attention to investigating the frosted tufts of grass. Snipe squatted by the frozen edges of the streams without having any 'visible means of sustenance.' The small finches alone were able to live comfortably on the seeds of grass and weeds. We fed as much as we could spare of corn and bread to the birds, but it was impossible to feed anything but the merest fraction of such an army. For the lapwing and golden plover, which seemed to suffer most, we could do nothing; they would not eat corn or bread.

On the fifteenth of the month, and after four days of intense frost, a heavy fall of snow covered the island more than a foot deep during the dark hours of the morning. It was fine, dry, powdery snow and was blown by the wind into drifts four or five feet deep. The high, open places were almost swept clean by the wind and the exposed ridges of the meadows were likewise swept. Here the birds sought for food in the face of the bitter wind and obtained almost nothing.

Probably most of the birds arrived on the island already in poor condition at this time, for at inland places on the mainland the snow had been much heavier and the cold more intense. At any rate this fall of snow on the island brought to our very door scores of weak and dying birds. It was saddening to find, on the day after the snowstorm, birds crowding for shelter into the farm fold and buildings, many barely able to fly more than a few yards.

Another day passed during which much of the snow had been blown away, but it was still freezing. The birds were now hand-tame through hunger and cold. Lapwings, unable to fly and barely able to utter a feeble call, tottered unsteadily behind the high walls of the folds. Golden plover were in worse condition, many dying at our door, whilst others crouched down on the very step. We carried some indoors, but the warmth of the room seemed to have an adverse effect on them, hurrying their death by a few hours. Each bird we carried in seemed to droop instantly – the transition from intense cold to the neighbourhood of a fire in a room proved too much for them. They breathed very quickly for a few moments, drooped their heads and died: lark, robin, starling, hedge sparrow and plover. We could do no more, though the birds seemed to be seeking our help in the way they crowded about the house, the buildings and the home meadows.

It was at this time that we had several tame rabbits living in outdoor pens, and the does were already busy rearing their young in the shelters provided for them. By day the hungry birds stole and fought over the rabbits' corn and roots, and at night they crept into the inner compartments of the hutches, nestling down among the baby rabbits and against the bodies of the does for the sake of the warmth. It was a strange sight to open a hutch and find the doe brooding a family consisting of her own furry offspring and a batch of perhaps six to a dozen starlings, thrushes or blackbirds. Sometimes a wren or a hedge sparrow would be there. In the mornings the birds would straggle out to face the world once more and seek food, but often they left their weaker comrades behind. Each day I had to remove a certain number of birds which had succumbed in the hutches overnight.

Farther afield, away from the buildings, the crows and gulls, at least, were not starving. They had plenty of victims for the trouble of knocking them over, though it is true that such fare was a scant one of feathers and bones, so miserably emaciated were their victims.

On the sea, when, on a calm day we crossed to the mainland, we saw several flocks of larks and starlings flying very weakly and low over the water. Many must have fallen into the sea on their voyages, unable to continue the exertion of beating their wings. Martynshaven beach was lined with dead birds. We saw one song thrush hovering over the water as if it thought to alight on an imaginary stone; there was no stone there, however, and the exhausted bird sank into the sea, to be drowned at once.

Even some of the robbers perished. We found several dead and dying herring gulls and two great black-backs, as well as many dead crows. We lost our beloved pair of stonechats, and it was not for a whole year that we regained a pair in their place on the island. One lady chaffinch, who had but one eye, lived comfortably at night in the corn bin, flying in when I opened the door, and in the morning she shared the chickens' food with Jonathan and Co., many starlings and small birds.

The weather broke early in March, at least enough to thaw the ground, and the sun shone often. The birds recovered strength with amazing celerity, and in a few days the feeble calls and tottering flight of the golden plover were changed to their normal sharp whistle and swift direct flight. The shearwaters, banished by the cold after an early arrival in February, returned in great strength. The oystercatchers rattled off their spring alarums, selecting the sites for their nests, each pair strictly to a well-defined territory of its own, on the high outcrops of rock in all the meadows.

Not many days later came the wheatears and an early chiffchaff, as well as that rarer visitor, the black redstart. Once more dread winter was over and sweet spring here again.

Often, when early spring had arrived, I had a great longing to see the old farm re-established on the island.

Fifty years ago, and probably earlier, Skokholm was farmed to a high degree of agricultural perfection. Witness the well-planned network of hedge walls and ditches, and the neatly arranged farm offices, now all tumbled down, save what we have restored for our own use.

The old-age pensioners on the mainland can remember the heyday of Skokholm's prosperity, when a bull, a stallion, rams and boars sired their respective herds and flocks in the fields and on the rough grazings. They remember the proverbial fatness of beasts carried or swum across from the island, the pools of water that stood in the hollows of their backs afterwards; the bacon was superlative; the cream for the butter so thick as to float an old Georgian penny on its surface. The grain grown was always sold for seed, the farmers' carts waiting eagerly for the boats as soon as the grain reached the mainland in them. Even the rabbits were so fat and prolific as to pay a high rent each year; no matter how thinly they were caught down it was always a problem to prevent them swarming into the growing corn in the summer.

Now, when I walk about the old fields and deserted outbuildings on calm days I have an idle fancy, a half-wishing, a half-expecting, that the trance-like stillness will be broken and the calls of the birds interrupted suddenly by the clatter of the farm life of old, that there will be neighings, lowings, bleatings, carts rumbling, scythes sharpening, maids singing at butter-making, labourers clattering over the stone walls to their noon dinner. I fancy I see the old sea captain who once farmed this island (indeed, retired sea captains generally farmed the Pembrokeshire islands in those days) walking about, superintending.

Would it be worthwhile to attempt a full restoration? I often ask myself, and sometimes I answer 'Yes.' I am always full of a desire to restore the old hedge walls to their former height and beauty, and my favourite pastime is stone hedging. But there are one or two problems to be solved.

In the old days labour was cheap and plentiful and easily accommodated: today it is difficult to obtain men willing to live permanently on a rather

inaccessible island. After a few weeks, perhaps a month or so, they grow
weary of island life, and long for village delights, vaguely imagining that
they are missing something, desirous of having weekends off and long
holidays ashore. I do not blame them; I merely state a fact which, most of
all, would handicap a scheme of reconstruction.

It is as well that I am no capitalist, else in my haste to have a farm on
the island I should probably destroy much of the peculiar charm which
lies in its wide-openness, its acres of luxuriant wild flowers, heather and
bracken stretching over field and cliff alike. Certainly many sea pies and
gulls would be driven out before the plough and harrow. By restoring
the hedge walls more puffins and shearwaters would have to take to the
already overcrowded cliffs. On the other hand, I sometimes think this
would be compensated for by the return of the arable-land birds. I should
welcome the corn bunting with his jangling bunch of keys. I should be
sure of partridges, and almost as sure of corncrakes, which love coast
meadows. Swallows and wagtails would return to the cowsheds. I should
have blackbirds and dunnocks about the garden. Perhaps robins, wrens and
song thrushes, enjoying the shelter of the new hedges, would be persuaded
to stay on and nest; at present they only winter here.

Indeed, I am torn between the desire to lead a simple pastoral life and the
wish to become a farmer. Each has many advantages and brings to mind
pictures rich in interest and beauty. Would the worry, the muck, the hard
work and the boating of heavy stock and plant involved in having a general
farm outweigh the benefits of being able to produce almost all our food, of
having an absorbing interest in the land at every season of the year?

How difficult farming would be was clear to me on the day we brought
a pony over in the *Foxtrot*. It took five men one hour to throw and tie
Punch in the boat, on a bed of straw. But he stepped ashore on the island
easily enough.

Now that his folk are growing older, our man John, to whom we owe
our apprenticeship in the ways of a small boat at sea, is required to help
with the garden and cows of his folk ashore. We have agreed together that
the summer fishing, though it has its excitements, is a hard living for two

men. So John goes off to dig the garden for his people, and spread manure, and chain harrow the smallholding fields (three cows and six acres). He will not be able to resist fishing on his own account with some 'mate' he can agree with in Marloes. He will spend a merry month at midsummer making hay for his folk and helping all his helpers to make theirs; finally, the equinoctial gales and ground seas will destroy his lobster pots in September. Then he is ready for his winter's work again. If we need him at busy times, such as shearing or boating of sheep, he is ready to spend a few days here, and the summer that Ann was born, and Doris much too engaged with the new arrival to partner me in the boat, he stayed on with us over the fishing season. Boy Henry left us after his one happy year pioneering and helping to get things straight before my wife came. He carried away with him a broader chest and an unappeased appetite for life on the High Seas.

Thus, alone on the island together, we have at last reached that complete independence we desired and planned for.

It has not been achieved without some travail of thought about ways and means. Since we depend on the island for our living, we have had to budget accordingly. Producing most of our own food, living simply, with plain tastes in food and clothing, with firing at the cost of our own labour only, our expenses are few, and are covered by the receipts from a flock of one hundred ewes and the winter's rabbit crop. These sheep are just a comfortable handful for one man who has regular assistance from his wife and occasional extra help from outside and from the keepers at the island lighthouse.

For heavy work the pony Punch, imported from the Welsh mountains, draws a light cart. And he is useful to ride around the sheep if I am in a hurry.

It was considered in the old days that, as a sheep run only, the island should produce a lamb an acre – that is to say, two hundred and fifty lambs – which would be the produce of not fewer than one hundred and seventy ewes of the somewhat light type kept locally. To increase now would mean hiring an extra hand. An extra hand has to be fed and housed. Doris says: 'Let's enjoy the island for a few more summers before we start to exploit it.' And generally I agree with this charming proposal to continue the idyllic life.

EIGHTEEN
Shepherding

B ECAUSE COLD WINDS and sweeping gales may still visit us in February
and March, we delay the lambing until All Fools' Day. Then in a spate
the curlycoats arrive, and gambol over new-flowering primroses, violets,
celandines and campion. This is one of our exquisite pleasures, this magic
privilege of walking round the island to attend these solicitous mothers
and their carefree offspring, when every stroll brings to view new flowers,
and hosts of sea fowl arrive, and streams of migrants pass.

By mid-April, bluebell time, most of the sheep have lambed and the
weather is mild enough for the rest to be born in comfort, almost without
anxiety on our part. It is astonishing how the later lambs will grow and
catch up with the earlier ones; they quite equal March lambs on the
mainland, which often suffer a setback during a cold spell. Lambing over,
what a profound satisfaction to watch the whole flock, ewes and lambs,
walking through the North Haven Bluebell Meadow early in May! I have

no wish to be anything but a shepherd in this sweet spring season.

But there are anxious days as well. Not all ewes are good mothers. By a good mother I mean an ewe which will not move more than a few feet away from her lamb during the first twenty-four hours after birth. It may not be generally known that a lamb requires and seeks nourishment as soon as it is born. So it must get on its feet at once. Well does the hill and moor shepherd know this. He keeps the careless ewes from wandering and strives to get the lambs upon their feet, realising that if they fail to get up within an hour of birth they seldom survive.

As long as his ewes are enclosed he can do this. But some ewes are very late, dropping their lambs after the flock has been turned out upon the summer grazings. Then he must watch the ravens.

One spring afternoon we got our flock into the fold, making a count of two hundred and one – that is to say, one missing. I went along the rocks in search of the truant. I soon found that the missing ewe had hidden herself among the razorbill ledges of Mad Bay and was about to give birth to a lamb.

I should not have found her if I had not first heard the ravens there. They are the ruthless midwives which attend these out-lambing ewes. They never let a weak lamb escape. (Yes, they have much to answer for, yet I would not be without their spring somersaulting, nor their aerial manoeuvres on dull February days.)

I crept down the jagged cliff. I could see the ewe angrily stamping a forefoot at the birds, which, bowing their heads and distending their throats, croaked so menacingly at her. The lamb was not yet born – not a sign – yet the ewe kept looking back tailwards anxiously and baaing with maternal solicitude. Presently, she lay down to begin her struggle. When one raven hopped nearer she got up bravely to stamp at it, but was obliged to lie down almost at once. This went on, between pains, until the lamb was born. The ewe instantly arose and, leaning down, began to lick her child dry, with an occasional fierce look and a stamping of one foreleg at the birds. They kept their distance, some four yards from her.

An oystercatcher, swerving close over my head, suddenly let off its deafening alarm, which sent the ravens and all else flying up. Even the ewe pricked up her head towards the sea pie, but seeing me coming down she went on quietly with her task.

I thought: 'A good mother; I'll keep her another year.'

The lamb was straddle-legged beneath her, sucking hard within five minutes of birth.

Someone once asked me if a starling on the back of a sheep is a sign of fine weather. It is more probably a sign that the sheep needs dipping. We find now that one strong dip before lambing, one after shearing, and one in the autumn, keep the ewes free of keds, scale and maggot (and, incidentally, of starlings and wagtails). The spring dip is also useful as a preliminary grease and dirt remover before the usual wash in May. Rubbing against and lying about in the sandy bird burrows and the stone hedges, the ewes gather a lot of grit into their wool. Lambs get a dip or two at midsummer and they take the bath with their mothers in the autumn. The rule is a cool day and a strong solution.

The goats never mingle with the sheep; not only do they ignore, but they never seem even to 'look towards' one another. If, as sometimes happens, we are rounding up both, the goats will range at a distance from the sheep, or occasionally they will be in the midst of them, but always with a wide space made around them, as if they mutually feared contact. I think that the goats dislike the sheep more than the sheep the goats. At any rate they appear to avoid them more deliberately, though this may be because goats are so much more active.

As soon as we let them out in the morning the goats go straight to the bog to sample the grass and herbage there. Then they chiefly range the cliffs and outcrops of rock, seeking the grey-green frosted lichen which covers these, and which is supposed to, and I think does, induce an abundant flow of milk.

We can rely on Matilda for a half-gallon of milk a day from March to September, the supply dwindling until she becomes dry by the New Year. Once her lactation period extended for eleven months. Katherine, a year younger, gives a pint a day less, while Biquette, younger still,

yields proportionately less. On the whole these figures do not compare
favourably with results from goats artificially fed and well cared for on
sheltered pastures, but they far surpass those of the native goats kept under
similar hard conditions on the mainland opposite.

A fawn-coloured Toggenburg strain, our goats contrast well with the
three black-and-white Welsh nannies kept by the lightkeepers. The two
tribes meet each day on the bog, and after wandering about together for an
hour or two, as if exchanging small talk (there is a good deal of bleating at
meeting), they usually disperse, and gradually – though alas! not invariably
– work their way home to their respective stalls by 7 p.m. – milking time.

When I first came to the island there was an ancient Welsh billy, William
the Conqueror, all horns, beard and temper, but my gentle Swiss billy
replaced him by an order in council. Two years later Rufus met with a
tragic end. He disappeared as if spirited away, and no amount of searching
of cliffs, afoot or by boat, could discover him. So he had to be replaced by a
young billy, Henry the First. Then one day, when breaking up a tree stump,
which the sea had wedged into a cave in North Haven, we found Rufus's
horns there too, sole relic of that brave spirit which once had ranged the
isle with decorous step, docile wives at heel.

NINETEEN

Ann

A NN CAME AFTER THE LAMBS IN MAY. Convenience dictated that she should be born on the mainland. Three weeks later I came over to fetch her and her mother. The *Storm Petrel*, shining with a new coat of paint, flew a pennon at bow and masthead. The day was calm, with hot sunshine struggling to dispel the morning vapour. A thousand bright-winged birds fluttered over the still sea, diving, swimming and fishing among the ripples of our wake. When we drew in towards the island harbour we were pleased to see it festooned with bunting. The flags spelt out a gay W-E-L-C-O-M-E in the International Code. The lightkeepers stood to salute us, and a cheer was raised as eager hands lifted the Princess's cradle ashore. Punch the pony was there, harnessed to carry her, still sleeping from the rocking of the boat, up to the house, above which the three code flags spelling her name stirred gently in the windless air. Our flagstaff had been made into a

Maypole, and later, when the mist cleared, all the flags danced to the tune of the north wind in the stay wires.

The first time we voyaged abroad with Ann the wicker cradle fitted nicely into the cockpit where the old engine used to be. In the early days, the movement of the boat nearly always sent her to sleep, but at times her eyes would be open and would be attracted by the kittiwake which often settled on the truck of the mast, or by the sweep of a gull passing overhead. A year later her little hands would be raised towards the bird, and the note of her perpetual wonder became 'Look! look!' Now that she is able to dispense with the cradle she sits and points out the birds to us, her eyes sometimes keener than ours. When the sea is calm she walks about with enthusiasm, steadying herself with her small legs to match the angle of the swaying boat; only in tide races and white wind-whipped water must she have the protection of someone's arms.

The sea greatly fascinates her, and it became in the first days a problem to circumvent her growing determination to study it from the landing steps in South Haven. But seeing me carrying a strayed sheep up a steep cliff one day, she became anxious for my safety, and so learned to value hers.

In time we gave her a pet lamb. Its name was Whisky. It was pure black in colour, one of twins, the other being pure white. They were born at the time of Ann's learning to walk. But Whisky never took her duties as crutch and companion seriously, and gladly made off at midsummer to take up the important position of sole black sheep in the island flock.

We wondered what colour her lamb would be in the next spring. But Whisky brought us two white lambs, as pure a white as the bells of the sea campion. Motherhood made her proud and fierce. No longer might Ann play with the black curls of Whisky's pate. The beautiful amber eyes seemed to shine with a mixture of jealousy and anxiety when we called her by name. She would run to the nearest hillock, calling and nosing her children, with backward glances.

TWENTY

Fishing

Like hayfever or chilblains, fishing is a seasonal disease. With the turn of every year the lobster fever seizes us. In February we say to each other:

'We shall fish this summer. Quite certainly.'

'It was a mistake ever to have given it up.'

I confess that in the seasons when we do not make a complement of pots I watch jealously the other boats round the island catching lobsters on our doorstep, or at any rate at our landing step. I forget the back-breaking pulling at oar and rope, the uncomfortable bumping in tideways, the stench of stale bait, the empty days, the storms that destroyed our pots, remember only the calm of sunlit days, when each pot held a wary crustacean and we basked with the puffins on the rippleless sea.

So I am always ready to start again. In March our fingers ache from twisting the withies. We collect the flat red pebbles of North Haven to make sinkers for the pots. We whittle baiting sticks. When the wildfowl go clanging northwards from our ponds we are in the midst of stretching the new-tarred ropes. Punch is harnessed to strain the heavy nine-strand lines we use for twenty-fathom work. When the swallows come we are piling the green cages high up on the little pony cart. Pots must soak three days before they will lie easily on the bottom of the sea. We sink them with extra stones in the shelter of South Haven for the required period.

To test the assertion that lobsters crawl most during the night, and are therefore most easily caught then, we spent one June night out in the boat. Well armed against the rigour of cold and appetite on the sea, with food and eiderdowns, we put in an extra large basket and plenty of seaweed, because we hoped we would need it. If, as other fishermen had told us, seventy lobsters were possible in a night's fishing, then our ordinary store box would soon be overflowing, and experience has taught us the discomfort of lobsters crawling in the bottom of a boat among feet and ropes.

'Shall we carry the engine?'

'Let us listen instead to the noises of the night birds on the water.'

We dipped oars in the molten-smooth sea, drifting with the strong north-stream tide to where our pots lay in the eddies at the Head. There was a bright moon and a clear sky, with the lights of ships on the edge where cloud meets horizon. For though the sky is clear, on the sea edge at night there is ever the appearance of a mist.

'They say that where we have put our pots today is the finest ground in all the islands.'

It was so bright that the shearwaters would not approach the cliffs. But the storm petrels were skimming like bats about us. It was very difficult to pick out our corks in the run of the sea. The light played tricks with the swirling froth of the backwater, so that slices of white foam in shadow were as black as buoys. Once we rowed up to a seal which, lying with eyes and nostrils at water level, simulated a buoy perfectly. Alarm having succeeded curiosity he dived with a velocity that sent a wash violently rocking the boat.

We did not find all the pots, but we hauled three strings, ten to each. When the first pot came up the moonlight revealed the glistening carapace of first one, then another, then a third lobster behind the prison bars of willow. As the next pot came dripping out of the water the light shone on the spines and warts of a crayfish. Now our hands were trembling. We said to each other that it was true then. We would soon have seventy fish.

But the next pot only had a little crab, the fourth pot two huge crabs, the fifth another crab, and the sixth quite empty. Thereafter we had almost nothing. A conger eel had slipped in and out of one string and devoured every piece of bait. When we had hauled all possible we reckoned five lobsters, one crayfish and twelve crabs. We had been out for two hours and were already hungry and tired. But we could not return at once. The stream still ran towards the north star, breaking against the side of the boat in luminous particles. We moored to one of our corks and huddled below the gunwale, eating our food in the warmth of eiderdowns.

We must have slept for at least some hours in our swaying cradle. The sun was on the horizon when we awoke, and a strange murmur in our ears. The current had long ago changed and, sweeping in our direction, had gently withdrawn the cork over the side of the boat, setting us free to drift over the smooth sea several miles from home.

We were close to a sister island, the steep cliffs of which were festooned with myriads of sea fowl – guillemots, razorbills, kittiwakes – whose clamour had roused us. Having swept us to the north, the current was now hurrying us to the south, and we were passing the seabird colonies at a rate that made the whole scene seem a moving panorama. We threw out our oars and pulled into a tiny fiord possessed by thousands of kittiwakes, whose cries made conversation difficult. From out of a deep cavern there swept a pair of red-billed, red-legged choughs crying 'Ki-ack! Ki-ack!' Above, a colony of cormorants were schooling in flying their young ones, who craned their snakish necks down at us in wonder.

We have since explored this island and know it now as a place of cliffs and caves, but, as poor islanders, our greatest discovery that morning was a hidden beach, at the back of the fiord and under a leaning brow of

Guillemots

rock, where we found the greatest mass of driftwood it has ever been our good fortune to behold. Rank upon rank, spars, beams, planks, hatches, stumps of masts, even whole masts, the whole beach was covered with timber. You might have thought that here the sea broke up privately all the old wooden ships that had yielded up their lives to her. No wind could blow the timber out to sea; the high cliffs screened off all but the prevailing sou'westers which, with the currents to help, had achieved this accumulation of centuries.

More than nibble at this great store we shall never do. The load we sailed home with that morning sank us to the gunwale, and lasted two months of bright fires.

We came often to this hoard, thinking of the winter, but however many loads we took we could make no mark upon it that gave us fear we should come to the end of it. For we now regard it as the timely successor of our coal supply. We have almost used up the last ton from the *Alice Williams*.

TWENTY-ONE
A walk around the island

WE HAVE JUST COME in with a northerly breeze and dropped our sail opposite the figurehead of the old wreck, the first person to greet us on entering the harbour.

To anchor in good holding ground we get the wooden lady in line with the whitewashed chimney of our cottage. This is South Haven: in this breeze the hottest place on the island and the best for a bathe. You can dive at any height from a range of steps and platforms which forms our landing quay, or you can walk in from the beach of bright red pebbles, from which in rough weather the boat is drawn up to a safe berth on the steep cliff above.

Having landed, you may take a pony tram and see the sights like any luxury-loving tourist, or you may walk. The tram line winds steeply near our cottage, passes the only tree on the island, *Salix repens*, which wisely lives by growing along the ground, rounds Tattenham Corner with a precautionary list inwards, and lands you in Puffin Town. A sharp rise follows, demanding a fair impetus. If you fail to surmount it you must get off and push behind. Be sure you get on again the instant the top is reached or you may find yourself empty handed! The pony knows the foibles of the track by heart, and dashes down the other side at full gallop to escape the tram that thunders behind him. Away the cavalcade goes, across the half-mile level plateau, through whirling clouds of nesting gulls, gradually sobering down to a steady trot as the line rises once more towards the lighthouse. This central plain is half bog, half pasture, and when we are gone, two by two, shoulder to shoulder, the amorous gulls settle down again, each pair to its inviolate square yard of territory.

We are on foot today, going slowly so that we can admire the untended wild garden, where a stream runs down to South Haven through banks of primroses (they flower from January to June here), cowslips, scurvy grass, arum, orchis, wild hyacinths, squill and celandines. We lie down a moment beside the water to catch its tinkle above the wash of the sea, for here, attracted by the cresses, dropworts and reeds of the stream, and the verdure of its banks, many migrants are resting and feeding.

The scented myriads of flowers are alive with willow warblers, chiffchaffs, grasshopper warblers, whitethroats and pipits, while above them hover migrant butterflies and resident bumblebees. On the naked slope above is a limekiln 'hung with sad mosses,' but they are not sad, these green-and-white tresses of sea campion and the yellow fingers of kidney vetch. This kiln is in perfect condition, with a heap of limestone broken fine for burning, though the last fire was drawn over fifty years ago. Now blackbirds and dunnocks nest in the bramble-grown crater, puffins in the flues, and in the heaped-up stones there is a thriving colony of those daintiest of birds, the storm petrels.

Northwards, over carpets of thyme, forget-me-not and violets, the island narrows to an isthmus scarcely seventy paces wide, forming the peninsula drably designated the Neck. It has never been ploughed and for centuries has been the province of the seabirds, which have fertilised it with their guano and castings; it is the richest virgin pasture on the island. Today it is a cloud of fire visible miles at sea and from the mainland, for the thrift has suddenly burst into glowing flames. Though scarcely twenty acres in area, it has a cliff line of more than a mile, beginning with Peter's Bay, where the seals love to lie basking at low water on south-facing reefs; Dumb Bell Bay, joined with the last by a natural doorway through arching cliffs, and leading down to the sheer pinnacles of the Devil's Teeth, below which (the fishermen say) so many wrecks lie rotting.

The side of one ship still lies in a deep cavern in the next cove, East Bay, where the corks of our pollack nets are bobbing. We must walk cautiously here: looking along the rising ground westwards a long line of ducks' heads peer at us over the clumps of heather and thrift. Every year a bachelor party of mallards settle on the Neck to moult into their eclipse plumage; when we first came only one pair, very wild, turned up; this year there are forty, so tame (though suspicious) that they are loath to rise. We avoid disturbing them, and so reach the last point of land eastwards near the mainland.

A narrow, current-swept passage separates us from the Stack, a tiny islet rising fifty or sixty feet, and crowned with flowers and purple sea tree mallows, among which those robbers, the great black-backed gulls, sit securely on their nests. Many pairs nest all over the island, choosing always a rock to anchor their nest against. To find them more easily we have successfully placed large stones in their favourite haunts.

More caves follow. One of these, yawning open in the grass, has defied all exploring efforts. The cliff here is margined with the nests of herring gulls, while inland are the widespread colonies of lesser black-backs. Between, the ground is a honeycomb of puffin burrows, through the thin crust of which our feet often step. Careful! Puffins resent intrusion with high courage and a formidable beak!

Next comes a tiny peninsula, mysteriously named Rat Island, which is occupied by five pairs each of puffins and storm petrels, three of herring gulls and one of great black-backs, oystercatchers and rock pipits. Here is North Haven, boasting the only sandy beach, and not too wide at that, yet large enough tor Ann to entertain her little visitors on. Here the buzzards nest, and about their steep home the cliff is hung with sloe, honeysuckle, privet, ivy, furze, hogweed, foxglove, bramble and hemp agrimony. On the left cliff we try the echoes; this and the hill behind the cottage give back clearly sentences of five or six words. The evening is best; by day the gulls make too much clamour.

Below this point a pathway, hewn in the solid rock, leads down to an old landing place; in strong, southerly winds we use it if South Haven is unapproachable.

Westwards the coast grows higher and wilder; huge pieces of cliffs have fallen to make the tumbled chaos so beloved by razorbill and petrel. On the steeper niches guillemots are ranked, and a perpetual groan comes up to us from their squabbling colonies. Standing thus we are overtaken by a flashing stream of swallows, martins and swifts. They are all crossing to Ireland, the fury of migration plain in their arrow-like flight. There is no deviation to feed, no loitering in sunny bays. Onwards they go, leaving us no longer amazed that they often overshoot their breeding grounds and appear in such places as St Kilda, Iceland and Spitsbergen!

On the Hard Point a pair of choughs are busy feeding. The long, curved bill serves as a pick for digging out the insect treasures of the thrift clumps. In Mad Bay the ravens are fledged, their parents are moulting – here is a fine black quill stolen to decorate the nest of a gull. Birds love decoration; this oystercatcher's nest is lined with shells and fine slices of red sandstone, not one larger than a shilling piece. The great black-backed gulls have adorned their nests here with the skulls and skins of their feathered victims. In North Haven the buzzard's nest is ever lined with fresh greenery, generally the flowers of campion and scurvy grass.

Many carrion crows nest on the island, acting as scavengers to the robber gulls; over there a great black-back has just killed a rabbit, while a pair of crows hop round picking up the morsels. They do it cleverly: while the gull drives off one, the other is tucking in behind its back; so that the gull would have a thin time if he did not in the end wisely carry his feed off to sea. Gull and crow hate each other. In a sheltered bay we surprise a pair of crows feeding a young one, which has got out of the nest rather early. As the crows rise at our intrusion a black-back swoops past the fledgeling, sending him spinning with a blow from his great wing. Furiously the parents chase the assailant, but the triumphant 'Hew, hew, hew!' of the gull has attracted others. Before we or the parents can get to the young one three other gulls have swooped at it. The last one taps it on the head with its flame-tipped bill. When we pick up the fledgeling it is quite dead. We shall leave it. No bird will touch the hateful meat, but before it is cold the bottleflies will have found it, and for the rest there are the eager burying beetles and the red and black ants.

Coming in over the hidden rocks of the Wild Goose Race the sea is never still in Mad Bay; the lower rocks are ever drenched in spray, the edges of the cliff hung with fern and lichen. Here sea and rocks unite in mad confusion, and in both the shining hosts of seabirds find safe cover. Farther on, the rocks are festooned with primrose-covered walks. We can imagine this to be the Love Lane of the days when a patriarchal sea captain lived here with five daughters, each of whom is said to have duly and without ceremony contributed to the thriving population of the island. A wilder, prettier spot for love-making could not be imagined.

Climbing now through a pasture full of squill and violets we reach the highest and most westerly point, the favourite perch for viewing the sunset over Grassholm and the lonely Smalls lighthouse, and for watching the dense multitudes of the shearwaters which glide together then, between island and island. Magic, changing carpets of jet and opal, they will not come inland until it is dark. Eager though they are to return to their sitting mates in the depths of the rabbit warrens, they seem to know that their nocturnal habits on land alone save them from total extinction by predatory birds. As it is they suffer hideously: everyone that does not find cover before light is massacred by the gulls; just here their wings and breastbones litter the cliff edge, their skulls peep out from clumps of thrift.

Now we are at the Head, which takes all the Gulf Stream can give after a four-thousand-mile sea run from the West Indies. Yet it is calm today; the fishermen are dropping their pots about the Long Nose, seeking the pale-blue lobsters that frequent the Head. Like the chameleon the lobster varies with environment. I have caught them around this island ranging in colour from navy-blue and indigo to the exquisite sky-blue of a dunnock's egg. On the Hard Point – so called because of the tangle of two steamers in collision which lie below and foul the fishing gear – the lobsters come up looking half-boiled, with the redness of rust.

Now we are at the lighthouse, very white and gilded without, with spotless floors and shining brasswork within. At night the red light says 'Keep clear,' and even the birds do not dash themselves upon the glass as they do under the fatal glare of the white beams of our neighbour the South Bishop, where bird rests have been provided.

We shall walk homewards along the top of the steep south cliffs, which below are a wilderness of terraces owned by herring gulls and razorbills, and above are a labyrinth of thrift clumps and burrows, where at nights thousands of shearwaters hold revel. Upreared among these are many sandstone outcrops. On windless nights, when these long-winged birds have difficulty in rising from the rough ground, they may be seen scrambling, their trembling wings arched angel-fashion high over their backs, up to the highest pinnacles, where they take off with a better chance of success.

Just here is the Iron Rock, in a niche above which our peregrines have their ancient eyrie, convenient to a bountiful supply of their favourite game, the unfortunate ubiquitous puffin.

All the while the chorus to every description herein should read 'and always the puffins, wheatears and pipits,' for we cannot escape them anywhere. Nor do we wish to. Now, passing Frank's Point, we are entering the great Puffin Metropolis, Crab Bay. Here on fine summer evenings, preferably with a little breeze to enable them to take the air more quickly, puffins in myriads promenade the turf, which is here finer than a bowling green, with dwarf and scorpion grasses, stonecrops and sea storksbill. Only, in their neat black coats, the puffins are more respectable than the promenaders at other coast resorts. If we go carefully they will not move until we nearly touch them. Looking at them closely we find that many have noticeably larger heads and thicker beaks than others – possibly these are old males – while one in about twenty has pale orange and not vermilion feet. These, perhaps, are older birds, which have lost pigment in the stress of the breeding season. I often ask myself, of what use is the enormous multicoloured bill? Since it is common to both sexes it is not male adornment, like a turkey's wattle or a redstart's gorget. Several pairs are engaged in rattling their bills together, castanet fashion, heads decorously bowed, as if to conceal somewhat these discreet overtures of courtship. When a third interrupts a happy pair he is instantly set upon by one of them. Locked in a flurry of legs and wings they roll over and over, bouncing down the cliff, to finish it out in and under the sea. In flying, the puffin spreads its webbed feet wide either side of its stumpy tail as an additional rudder to steer by in banking, stalling and turning movements.

Through thick cushions of heartsease pansy, wild thyme, speedwell and wood sage we climb upwards to the naked height of Spy Rock. From this point the old farming captains used to watch their hands at work in the fields. What would they say now to see their hedges tumbled down, their fields an open refuge for the birds and beasts they spent all their days driving therefrom? An old woman on the mainland tells me that her father used to keep watch all night when the corn was growing, sending his four daughters out in relays to beat the boundaries and drive the sheep and conies back into the rough grazings. From here everything is spread before us, the south pond, where our turbary is; the bog, in the cool long grass of which the pony and goats are enjoying their noon siesta, and the water of the north pond, alive with gulls, who all day come to wash the salt of the sea from their plumage, with mallard, teal, snipe and rail for company.

Let us leave Spy Rock to the gulls, whose nests fill the nooks of its jagged height, and continue eastwards into Wreck Cove. Here at low water we shall see the anchors, chains and metal parts of the last two wrecks tangled amid the giant red boulders. Though the coal we stored from the *Alice Williams* is now running low, some of her gear still lies high and dry near by, a dwindling treasure trove of ships' fittings, among which the gulls and razorbills have laid their eggs.

The Ebbing Stone, appearing at half tide, is the fishermen's guide for taking the north-going current home, and our boundary in swimming. None but the seals can stem the furious tide rip that lies south of it.

Next comes Boar's Bay, hung with hemp agrimony and dropwort, and so, passing the figurehead, we come back to harbour again.

TWENTY-TWO

Summer

WE HAVE TWO LARKS singing on the island. They begin long before sunrise, but not before the oystercatchers are awake and trilling their loud reveille: 'Awake! Awake! Wake, wake, wake. . .'

From midnight until 2 a.m. the shearwaters utter their unearthly screams, quite drowning the soft crooning notes which come from the storm petrels nesting in the hedges and walls. Impossible to describe the shearwaters' call – beyond hinting that it suggests a catcall and a cockcrow uttered simultaneously and cut off with a sharp knife before the finish. At two-thirty 2.30 a.m. the wheatears exchange a few sharp notes. Then Jonathan, our Rhode Islander, gives out his fine challenge, though there is no other cock to answer him. Soon the sea pies wake up from their uneasy sleep and rouse our world with their clamour. The gulls begin complaining and the larks go up to heaven.

When from the low window we see the sun shining on a placid sea, barely rippled by the headstrong tide, when all the far headlands are bathed in the strong light, we too are invigorated. It may be that there is not a breath of wind to rustle the purple sea spurrey growing on the lintel. The loveliness of the world enchants us; we grow excited. Or it may be that the fine weather tempted us to sleep in the heather. How eagerly we rush down for the morning dive in the harbour! How impatient are the goats to be milked and freed from their night stall!

We sing as we lay breakfast outdoors. We hasten to wash up afterwards and to finish all the tiresome household duties. Then comes the consideration of the day's work. Is it a Grassholm day? No, there is still the faintest wash of white foam, legacy of the last storm, at the base of the higher cliffs. A landing on Grassholm is possible only when no swell whatever is visible. 'Grassholm days' are so few that we have to look out for and seize each opportunity.

The programme is soon laid out. I am to cut peat in the morning while Doris does some necessary housework, including the making of one of her incomparable rabbit pies. We are to fish in the afternoon to replenish a depleted larder.

The coal from the wreck of the *Alice Williams* having dwindled to the last few tons, we save these for special baking days and for very cold weather. With care, this remnant should see us beyond another winter. The island 'peat,' which is really little better than consolidated layers of turf, burns well, if quickly, with a deep-hearted glow, and with a log of driftwood to make a bright flame is splendid in the capacious grate of the living room. Even when we are out of coal, Doris proposes to cook with peat in the old-fashioned way. Of course there is plenty of driftwood, and, as usual in summer, we have accumulated a great pile, ready for the winter fires.

Spade on shoulder I go out to dig my turves on the island bog, and spread them out to dry. They have then to be stacked to dry, and are finally taken home, to go under cover, with Punch in the light cart assisting.

The surface of the 'turbary' supports a light growth of thrift and bog pimpernel. As I cut out the cubes, spade-deep, four inches wide, a pair of oystercatchers fly angrily above my head, calling: 'Keep still! Keep still!'

They are warning their three downy young ones, which pretend to be invisible, crouching under a pile of my turves. For the two hours that I ply my spade they keep still in their shady hiding place, while I perspire in the sun. At last I consider their probable hunger and cautiously withdraw them from their hole. They scream vigorously. Their parents, hitherto dozing uneasily a few yards away, at once fly up and scream loudly. The gulls take up the alarm and soon the whole bog is in an uproar.

All the blame falls upon a heron which happens to be passing. The gulls, the lapwings and the sea pies together make an attack upon him. In his unwieldy fashion the big grey bird turns and twists in an endeavour to avoid his more formidable assailants, the great black-backed gulls. He calls out his distress in a deep, hoarse voice. I have long ago allowed the young sea pies to run off to their parents, and am busy spreading the cut turves out to dry before the clamour subsides. The heron is driven off the island altogether, and heads for Grassholm, still pursued by a frantic gull.

At noon it was cooler, a breeze coming out of the west. I was very hungry, and dined greedily off rabbit pie, new peas and potatoes, followed by stewed rhubarb and junket, everything home-produced, like the goat's milk we had with our morning porridge. Then I weeded in the garden for an hour, and afterwards went out to sea with Doris to haul two dozen lobster pots. Fairly good result: one crayfish, two small lobsters and five crabs. We also had a giant conger eel in one pot, but could do nothing with it, so saved it to give to the lightkeepers. Thousands of puffins, guillemots and razorbills were diving for sprats in the harbour, while the kittiwake gulls snatched those feeding on the surface. Whence came these myriads of sprats at such an opportune time to feed all the young broods in July and August? We fished with lines for another hour, but caught only a mackerel and two pollack.

And so to tea, strawberries and cream, brown bread and lemon curd, and cake. The strawberries we manage to grow in a sheltered corner of the garden are few but fine; the curd Doris makes from fresh gulls' eggs in season.

The goats and the sheep have often an inconvenient habit of moving along the coast all day as they browse and ending up at the far end for the night, a mile from the house. We agreed to round them all up tonight, but that on our way we would put numbered rings on the legs of one hundred razorbills. Razorbills are likely to be profitable. A number ringed as nestlings in July in Scotland were recovered on the Scandinavian coast in November – a curious migration.

The west wind had increased to nearly a gale as we walked over to Mad Bay, where our greatest colonies of razorbills hide their eggs and downy young. Down among the boulders and talus of the bay we searched. Beneath the red rocks the handsome black-and-white adults stood guard over their one solitary youngster. The oldsters growl alarmingly at you, while the babies squeak in a high, thin pipe. It is not easy to corner the old birds; they make a dash for safety if they see their chance. Even when caught they bite severely – as our wrists soon testified – with their sharp razor bills. We managed, nevertheless, to ring at least a dozen adults.

'Grr . . . rr!'

'Quick, I've got one! A ring, please!'

A ring is quickly clipped on one leg, its number noted, the bird released. The young ones were easy to ring, and we went along at a fine pace, for they were plentiful under every piece of broken cliff.

The tide and wind had been steadily rising. The smooth water of a calm summer day was now transformed into a series of giant swells, which, rank after rank, flung themselves on the worn red cliffs and into the deep caves, throwing the spray ever higher and higher. The setting sun shone brightly and threw a bow into every tall column of spray. The lowermost razorbills were anxious about their young ones; those with eggs were safe, but the heavy spray ran back in streams over the cliff, and many a baby we found sitting in a pool, cold and numb.

The adult razorbills sitting on the tops of the lower rocks made the prettiest scene when they flew high up in the air all together each time a high wave threatened them, mingling delightfully with the spray and the rainbows against the background of red cliff, with its green thrift and yellow lichen.

There was so much to find and see that evening that the sun set long
before we were ready for it. We came on a valuable piece of timber wedged
in the rocks, to say nothing of firewood. We found hundreds of other
birds, nests, eggs and young. We trembled when we came across the young
gulls who were grown enough to be able to walk confidently to the edge,
ready, heedless of their lives, to take the plunge into the raging sea if we
approached a foot too near. A tiny storm petrel was brooding its egg in
an unexpected position, in the centre of a flat stretch of wind-blown sand
beneath high boulders. A young shearwater was cunningly placed in a slit
in a rock. Here and there were crowded bunches of guillemots, their once
bright green eggs thickly bedaubed with the muck of the colony. A few had
hatched, however, just to prove that the coating of filth made no difference
to successful incubation.

That evening we were lucky enough to see a seal feeding. In a narrow
creek out of the wind, where the backwash from the waves nevertheless
made angry white water, a huge dark seal – it must have been an old bull –
had just caught a giant brown skate, and was doing battle with it. The fish
was fully three-fourths the length of the seal, if the long tail be included,
and a good deal wider. The seal had gripped the skate in the vital spot in
the centre of its white underside, and although the fish now lashed the seal
furiously with its tail, and anon struck blows with its wide 'wings,' the
issue was scarcely in doubt. Placing its two paws tightly around the skate,
and gripping it with extended claws, the seal tore the mouthful he already
possessed completely out of the fish and, tossing up his head, swallowed
it with a few gulps. Again and again he tore and swallowed. The skate
struck with its tail less and less frequently: it threw its tail around the
seal's thick neck, as if in an endeavour to strangle the monster. When the
fish was too weak to escape, the seal began playing with it, tearing out a
mouthful and then letting the skate swim feebly away while it swallowed
the morsel; then it would dive after its victim, bring it to the surface for
another bite and let it sink again, and so on. Though it was torn to ribbons
underneath, the skate still showed life in its feebly thrashing tail and fins.
We felt compassion for the dying skate, and forbore to witness the last

disintegration. Chiefly, I marvelled that the seal could feed and play in such a wild backwater of the Atlantic, with white foam constantly washing over him.

The sun had long set when we actually used our last ring and came to the end of the more accessible colonies in Mad Bay. It was long past milking time, but we had spent a happy evening, and as we drove home the goats we felt tired.

'Tomorrow will do,' we agreed, looking at the sheep comfortably chewing the cud in a sheltered bay, and we did not disturb them that night. In the sky the new moon was very low. Doris bowed three times. She always does.

While I was milking I heard the night birds coming in. When the moon had set, the first shearwaters came screaming home. Then the breeding cry – I suppose really the love song – of our well-loved storm petrels. It is not often they are heard on the wing, and here was one flying round and round about the goat house. I put down my pail and ran to fetch Doris. Together we watched the little birds flying, calling, and chasing each other in their excitement. Their tiny forms loomed but faintly in the dark, but we saw them well when they brushed past our faces, forgetful or heedless of our nearness.

TWENTY-THREE

Birds and beasts

OUR ISLAND LIES BEYOND any point of land. There is no guiding cape or finger of land jutting towards it, as with the sister islands of Skomer and Ramsey. For this reason every bird that visits us is a true migrant, not a day visitor on the forage. Rooks, daws and starlings find it convenient to slip over to Skomer for the day, but if they come to us they come to stay, or else to pass on at once to the next refuelling station in the great migration merry-go-round. (It is now proved that a large number of species return in the spring by a different route from that used in the autumn.)

In winter I have my own starling roost. Each night I mark my starlings hastening to the razorbill ledges on the cliffs near the Stack. They go there before sunset and wheel about a great deal before settling down. The smaller passerines roost in deep heather and dead grass; wrens and hedge sparrows creep into rabbit holes or the deserted nests of the storm petrels. The coast is left clear for the night-feeding population.

Snipe leave the bog grass in hundreds and come to feed by every rill and damp corner, and with them many woodcock and curlew and grey and green plover. The widgeon come whistling in from nowhere, with quacking mallard and teal, until the ponds are black with their troops, and the water as muddy as a burn in spate. Not a square yard of the ground about the main pond but is trampled and printed by a thousand webbed feet, for by now the birds must know that our island is their only sanctuary in a noted game county. All night they feed and tread over the bog; in the morning I go out and marvel at the evidence, and my delight is even greater when I see the broad-web imprints and the grass-green droppings of the wild geese. Little owls are abroad too, and many water rails, both species capable of raising weird cries in the depths of the night, as well as by day.

The birds give us a pleasure that is at once possessive, friendly and absorbing. The joy of possession is emphasised on an island; every bird that flies to our shores is instantly labelled ours, no matter if it merely rests a moment and then flies on. In this way we have emissaries in all countries north, south, east and west of us. We often hear of the arrival of some of these ambassadors, when the birds we have ringed are reported in France, Spain or Morocco.

As for the resident birds, such as the ravens, falcons and buzzards, stonechats, dunnocks and pipits, they have long learned that we are harmless – merely a pair of clumsy, flightless *homo sapiens* nesting in the old house on the island. In winter, small birds constantly enter the house, often for shelter, more often, I suspect, out of a hungry curiosity. In summer, the starlings scutter about the eaves, pretending they will nest, but always flying away in the end to more civilised parts. The swallows, however, stay and build, as do the pied wagtails. At night, the slates are visited by amorous shearwaters, whose caterwauling and claw scratching is an imitation of what goes on on suburban roofs. I have already described Mr Puffin, who has increased of late years until he has now colonised the whole island. His townships number among them over 40,000 population. A decent, sober bird this, who goes to bed with the sun and gets up reasonably early, but for all that one who can enjoy a good laugh. Or so it seems to the human observer; for one after another a whole colony of puffins, some deep in their holes, will begin a throaty, aldermanic chuckle, 'Ah . . . ha . . . ha.' It rolls around from one colony to another, in and out of the holes, and is often taken up by puffins resting on the sea, so that you never seem to hear the end of what must have been an amazingly satisfying piece of puffin humour.

There have been rare exceptions to the rule of migrants and residents only. The tree creeper which visited us in July could only be called an adventurous wanderer. Discovering no trees, it used the rough granulations of the cliff in South Haven as it would the bark of a tree, and seemed to find insects aplenty in the crannies. A coal tit in December was equally adventuring; it was the only tit that has ever visited us. It stayed many days, finding chrysalids and spiders under walls and eaves. The golden-crested wren in October may have been a true migrant – for I have seen them on Grassholm – but it was a very fragile atom to be clinging to the bracken stalks in a high wind.

A lesser whitethroat was both a record-maker and a lost soul in a November storm, months after its kin had reached Africa. A northern guillemot which was found in the home meadow, a quarter of a mile from the sea, had dropped there out of sheer exhaustion in a gale, having long been suffering from oil waste on its plumage.

Twice now in the spring have sparrows looked in on us, ambitious cocks which have chirped in vain for mates to join them, and finally retired in despair. Once a wood pigeon flew in upon us. Its manner betrayed alarm and bewilderment, as well it might, for what had we to offer the fat, sleek creature of trees and corn and clover? It flew off quickly – I hope before our falcons saw it.

Another bird of the forest was the crossbill that perched on the garden wall one morning in July. There had been an invasion of the British Isles by this species, one of those periodic waves of emigration caused by over-population in Europe, and this solitary bird represented the farthest west achieved in England and Wales. The meadow pipits which nested in the garden were furious about the strange-looking bird, and chased it right off the island.

A sparrowhawk in August found good hunting among our small birds, and, uninvited, stayed the month out, taking up quarters in North Haven. In like manner, but far more welcome, a white owl came to spend November with us, and rid us of some of our mice. It was almost hand-tame, and quickly made a good impression by clearing the mice out of the Wheelhouse and occupying it instead. Then one day it vanished (returned to the mainland, I supposed), but later I found its dismembered corpse beneath a pile of wire netting. Had it got entangled, or had it died of a surfeit of mice? At any rate, the mice had their revenge on the body, having torn every vestige of its tough flesh from the bones and the feathers! (They devour almost anything in the winter, and are particularly fond of the composition buttons of our oilskins.)

The little ortolan which came to us in June was quite exhausted and did not at all remind me of a gourmet's delicacy. For a long time it took refuge in that ornithological holy of holies, our garden, until at last it was strong enough to fly out again into the sky, whither, who can tell? I know the charming little wanderer took with it something of our hearts.

In most springtimes one, and sometimes two, hoopoes visit us. Restless tropical bird, the hoopoe is not still for one moment, flying here and there, and at each alighting throwing erect its wonderfully coloured crest. To visualise this beauty, imagine the progeny of a jay mated to a great spotted woodpecker, for the hoopoe has the brilliance of both, and the size and swooping flight also. I would follow it from rock to rock about the island, but as a rule it would not accept my eager advances, but would fly down below the inaccessible cliffs, where I could not follow.

These are the strangers of note that have wandered to our lonely shore. A few sedentary, tree-loving species have never ventured so far. Hungry for all birds, we miss the titmice, all varieties, and the magpies and jays which abound on the mainland of Wales. The magpies come as far as Martynshaven in winter, but will not cross the sea, nor will any of the woodpeckers, although these species have travelled to the edge of Jack

Sound. However, when I look through the long list of species which I have recorded on the island, I feel I cannot grumble at the absence of a few old friends. Have I not a unique selection to take their place, a special migration of white wagtails, black redstarts, whimbrel, bar-tailed godwits, little auks, and sooty shearwaters, which is not observed on the mainland?

Turning now to the small beasts which inhabit the island, it is somewhat surprising that we do not possess mole, vole, or shrew. In common with many another island, Skomer has a vole peculiar to itself, differing in size and dentition from the common field vole. I am glad we haven't one, though if I listened to all my acclimatisation-mad friends, the island would by now be a miniature Whipsnade, bristling with voles, moles, shrews, badgers, foxes, martens, wild cats, hedgehogs, even snakes and guineapigs. I have had to refuse sanctuary to whole menageries of people's pets. Good heavens! Badgers would spend their nights digging out puffins and shearwaters, foxes would devour my rabbits, hedgehogs would suck the birds' eggs, moles would swallow up my scanty supply of worms, and voles are notorious for spoiling good pasture. As for shrews, I sometimes think we will sail over to Lundy Island and catch a few of the pygmy variety which inhabit this our nearest land to the southeast. Yet am I nervous of taking the plunge, for although shrews live on slugs, woodlice and earwigs, they may also fancy my newts and nestling birds.

The introduction of mice has been a grievous thing as it is. *Mus musculus*, common house mouse, voracious villain, was brought to the island accidentally about thirty years ago. The then tenant of the island wished to carry a colt over from the mainland and overnight prepared his boat at Martynshaven, laying down a great bed of straw for the young animal to rest upon. Here the method of carrying heavy stock in a boat is first to throw them in upon their backs, with the four legs tied together. Four men are needed, one to hold the head, one to hold a noose round the forelegs, one a noose round the hindlegs, and a fourth to place a stout plank under the belly and resting on the gunwale of the boat alongside which the animal is first placed. The man with the plank, at a word, levers the beast up, so that it rolls over into the boat upside down, the nooses automatically drawing tight. The beast is not allowed to raise its head from the straw until the four legs are lashed together. As a rule it lies very quietly on its bed, unless the job has been done in a slovenly manner as happened on one notable occasion, when a horse going to Skomer freed one leg and kicked the side of the boat out for its master.

It is a wonder that rats, as well as mice, were not imported by that negligent farmer who left his boat packed with straw on Martynshaven beach on that fateful evening. An eyewitness has since told me that when, the next day, they unloaded the boat in the harbour of our island, the colt, in getting up, kicked the straw about until several mice darted out and were lost immediately in the crannies of the island cliffs. In three years they colonised the whole island, spreading to every corner; in summer living a life of plenty in the pastures; in winter suffering from hunger, cold and flood, save those – and they come in scores – which fatten on our crumbs.

Rats swarm on Lundy and on Ramsey, and on many lonely islands. They are said to have come there from wrecks. I wonder. Skokholm and Skomer have had scores of wrecks, yet never has a rat landed. When I ask the fishermen why, they speak of rats forsaking a vessel long before she founders. They also tell a tale about the only rat known to have reached Skokholm. As it sprang from the boat on to the island beach it was slain with a pebble cleverly aimed by the outraged farmer; and they declare that it was a narrow squeak in more ways than one, because the creature proved to be a gravid doe!

Seals, rabbits and mice are our wild mammals, and I must add another, for at rare intervals we see a minute bat fluttering about, so insignificant that I think it must be a whiskered bat. Once only, on a still summer evening, did a pipistrelle venture across the ocean to us.

There are no snakes, but on fine days we see slow worms basking in the sun, especially on the hot slopes of South Haven. Finally, there are newts and frogs to complete the indigenous stock. Both I have had examined in the vain hope that they might be a race peculiar to the island.

Toads and lizards are on the list of creatures to be imported at every opportunity as harmless, nay, beneficial.

In Elizabethan times our island was famed for its 'great store of conyes,' as it is now and doubtless ever will be. For one thing, there are no stoats or weasels to decimate them. All interference comes from above, gulls devouring many young rabbits; the puffins and shearwaters do little damage: they only cause inconvenience by occupying the burrows in the height of the rabbit-breeding season, from March to August. After that the rabbits have things all their own way underground. So much so indeed do they rely on safety below ground that nothing will induce them to bolt. I have experimented with every sort of humane contrivance for catching them, in an endeavour to find a substitute for the steel trap. Pumping poisonous gas is an effective, but too expensive, method of extermination – the rabbits dying in the depths – 'at their posts,' so to speak. Muzzled ferrets failed to move the rabbits. They came up with their claws full of rabbit fur; they had been scratching the backs of the insensate conies!

At first thought this might seem to be utter stupidity on the part of the rabbits; but it is the opinion of the local rabbit-catchers that our island rabbits are, on the contrary, more cunning than the mainlanders, and are capable of staying in their burrows without moving for two weeks if they hear and smell traps being laid outside. As for all the humane snares and contrivances, I have tried every one, and so far have not been able to catch more than an occasional rabbit, the fault being that they are all too clumsy and conspicuous, an insult to a coney's intelligence in fact. Fine-wire snares, laid in the grass and heather, are fairly effective. Steel traps I would not employ again – they are neither economic nor humane.

The rabbit burrows here are the scene of great competition from February onwards. No sooner has the rabbit in February begun seriously to consider nesting operations than the shearwater arrives in the burrow. The island rabbit, which varies somewhat from the ordinary mainland rabbit in that it is smaller and has slightly darker and longer fur, does not begin to breed very early. Then, in April, the ubiquitous Mr Puffin arrives, demanding his share of the burrow.

It is a source of wonder to me where the doe rabbit actually hides her young. Most of the newly weaned young ones appear from holes which are definitely known to harbour shearwaters or puffins or both. Somewhere in the labyrinth below the doe must have found a corner in which to make her nest. First she tears mouthfuls of coarse grass and carries this below, next she lines the grassy nest with her own fur, torn from belly and breast so as to bare her teats for suckling. Here the naked, blind babies are hidden, the doe plucking more fur to cover them deeply. Finally, she covers the entrance to the nest burrow with more grass, and often with earth, so heavily that one might expect the babies to be stifled. Once in twenty-four hours, or possibly twice, she opens the nest to feed them, closing it again while they are still blind and helpless during the first nine days. After this period the young ones open their eyes and begin to scramble about, having already grown a thick brown baby coat, and a few days later they learn to run to the mouth of the burrow and nibble grass for the first time.

The doe forgets her first family when they are three weeks old and prepares a new nest for the second family. Her fecundity is amazing. After the first family in March, she has at least two and generally three more at monthly intervals, in April, May, June and even July. If she is a strong doe in her prime she may breed as many as five litters of four young ones in each, or twenty in the season. The March-born rabbits themselves breed before they are three months old, the does having one family in July or August. The April-born may also breed once in the same summer. The number of young in litters born to these young does is invariably very few, generally but two, occasionally three and rarely four. The old does will sometimes have six in one litter, often five, but usually four.

The mainland doe rabbit often makes her nest in a specially dug shaft a few feet long, the entrance to which she blocks with earth and turf. This for her is a wise precaution against marauding stoats and weasels, but is not necessary to the island doe, which seems to follow this procedure but rarely. As I have said, there are no stoats or weasels, in fact nothing more harmful than mice, frogs, newts, and slow worms in the way of creeping animals, on the island.

From the birds, however, the rabbits have to suffer somewhat. They are liable to have their noses or tails severely tweaked by the puffin's sharp beak, or to be held and wrenched by the shearwater's long, hooked bill, should they encounter either of the birds below ground, as they must frequently do. The shearwaters in particular are the usurpers of the burrows the rabbits have dug for themselves, for they follow the windings of the warrens to their farthest depths. They occupy the burrows until every available recess is engaged by a pair. On more than one occasion two pairs of shearwaters have occupied the same recess until one has been able to assert its right by laying the egg before the other pair did; and even then we noted an instance where a third bird brooded the egg belonging to another pair. Numbered rings which we placed on the legs of the birds enabled us to make this interesting discovery. On another occasion we found a shearwater brooding, or rather sitting, on top of a nest of blind young rabbits.

The puffin can drive away a rabbit by worrying it with its sharp beak, and almost all the short burrows and blind shafts within easy distance of the sea are occupied by Mr Puffin, to the exclusion of the rabbits and of most of the shearwaters. Many of the latter, however, occupy burrows opening upon, or near, those of the puffin, and as a result the two species not infrequently come up against each other in a battle royal. I have heard them scrapping below ground, and twice have I seen them come rolling out of the burrow, locked in a flurry of wings and legs, and stabbing, wrenching beaks. Once out in the daylight the puffin flew away into the sunshine as befitted a bird active all day, whilst the shearwater, a night-lover, hastened back to the gloom of the burrow, incidentally carrying off the honours of war.

Altogether, the overcrowding below ground is amazing, and productive of endless curious incidents, both grave and gay. For instance, a puffin incubated a shearwater's egg for a few days on one occasion until the egg got broken. The puffin then deserted it, leaving the burrow and its broken egg to the unfortunate shearwater. I have also a record of a puffin routing out a nest of newly born rabbits from a short burrow. The poor babies were found crawling at the mouth of the burrow, and soon made a meal for a hungry gull.

All these three dwellers underground have a common enemy in the gulls. As I have recorded elsewhere, these marauders search all day for young rabbits, and are equally ready to pounce on an unsuspecting puffin emerging from its burrow. Of the three gulls the herring gull is the mildest offender. Most of these confine their activities to fishing at sea, but a few depraved individuals earn an easier living by preying upon the inmates of the burrows, and by robbing the guillemots and razorbills of their hard-sought-for fish and, where possible, of their eggs.

A fourth invader of the rabbit burrows is the storm petrel, which arrives at the end of April. This little fellow, however, in no way incommodes the other burrow-dwellers, but rather keeps out of their way, using only the small holes and crevices at the mouth of the burrows in which to nest. The majority nest in crevices in hedge walls and cliffs. Like the shearwater, the storm petrel spends well over a month – actually thirty-eight days – incubating its solitary egg, which it lays late in May, or June, and then two months in rearing the nestling, so that we sometimes find a late youngster still in the nest in November.

TWENTY-FOUR

Experiments

EVERY YEAR FAVOURABLE WINDS bring us butterflies and moths – blues, browns, yellows, admirals, peacocks, cinnabars, burnets, tigers and hawks – all welcome enough; but it was unfortunate that the coming of cabbage butterflies coincided with our experiment of raising kale on a large scale.

In order to feed a small stud of Chinchilla rabbits, with which we were experimenting at that time, we had enclosed and planted half an acre of the home meadow with green stuff. There had been at first an idea that we could devote the island to the production of Chinchillas entirely, by getting rid of the wild rabbits; but on second thoughts it was realised that this plan was unsound, delightful as it would have been. Apart from the difficulty of exterminating the wild rabbits in their labyrinthine burrows, and particularly in their fastnesses in the boulder-strewn cliffs, it was remembered that Chinchilla skins are worthless unless taken at the right moment – that is, as soon as the winter coat is perfect; therefore it would be necessary to have the animals under daily scrutiny. In any case, the slump in prices for skins came just as we acquired the stud. We decided to use our animals solely as a means of improving the wild stock.

By turning down all that we bred in two years we succeeded in doing this. Whereas the natives normally average 4lb a couple, the hybrids frequently weigh 8lb a couple. They all revert to the wild stock in coloration, except for a bluish tinge in the short hair behind the ears, which are larger and blunter than in the wild rabbit; indeed, the result is a handsome animal.

In this half-acre of rabbit garden, which we spade-dug ourselves, were planted things beloved of conies – giant dandelion, spinach-beet, milk thistle, chicory, white turnip, kohlrabi, clover and vetches, cabbage and thousand-head and marrow-stem kale. Just to see how they would grow, we added a few perches of Great Scot potatoes and a strip of black spring oats.

What a joy that garden was! It became a paradise for the small birds on migration, and I risked a wetting daily by striding among the great cabbages to see what would fly up, willow warbler, whitethroat, sedge warbler, or landrail. We had only turned the sod over late in April, yet the kale, transplanted from the garden between showers in June, shot up waist-high. We reaped a thousandfold, more than twice our requirements. The oats were the finest grown in Pembrokeshire, if I am to believe one of her keenest farmers, who saw the narrow strip of breast-high grain. The potatoes were huge – veritable monsters. But the whole garden was a delight, from the first patch of dandelions to the last corner where the tall blue-flowering stems of chicory danced in the wind.

Then, one fine day, in a long procession, the butterflies began arriving out of the east on a warm breeze from the land, a quivering white thread never ending for two days. We found many washed ashore as well, so that thousands must have perished westwards in the sea and at Grassholm. They revelled in nuptial dance over our greenery while we looked on in alarm. We did make an attempt to collect the eggs, which were laid under every leaf, and a still more energetic attack on the young lame, but the search was too exhausting. The lighthouse gardens were quite denuded of greens, and it was surprising how well our great kale bushes withstood the attack of the myriads of caterpillars, shooting out branches and new hearts above the old leaves, which were reduced to skeletons.

The next stage was the march of the fattened caterpillars in search of winter quarters. In the still autumn days we could hear the incessant small scratching and creeping through doorways, up walls, along ceilings, under slates, while the windows were filmed with the fine yellow silk which these overfed grubs secrete wherever they go.

But Nature had already made her countermove, and very few became chrysalids. Instead we saw, with a gruesome pleasure, the grubs of the parasitic fly *Microgaster glomeratus* emerging at all points from the skin of the unfortunate caterpillars, which shrivelled up at once, while the guests wrapped themselves in gold silk for the winter.

We had no invasion from overseas the next year, with the result that these tiny flies had matters all their own way, and scarcely a caterpillar survived to the imago stage to lay eggs for the second brood that summer.

In the third year, as we had by then put all the Chinchillas to grass, we did not dig the rabbit garden, but let Nature have it for her children. The dandelion, chicory, kale, etcetera, ran wildly to seed amid seas of groundsel and flowering grasses, and we were rewarded with the prattle and songs all day long of the linnets, goldfinches, greenfinches and corn buntings. Even now the chicory and groundsel persist and the linnets come to feed all through the year.

As I come nearer to the end of this little book I look back on the latest records of the island birds and beasts. We love to study and experiment with these subjects of ours. But I find the birds have been very whimsical this year. More than half of my prepared nesting sites have been deserted.

I took a pane out of the Wheelhouse window to give the swallows free entry; but they built their nest in a little wooden hut in which we store the pony's hay. I made a number of holes in the garden walls and placed heaps of stones with dug outs beneath them for the storm petrels; they laid instead beneath a disused door, in a butter box, and under a peat hag. I scythed the bracken about the wall to discourage the whitethroats, which had ousted the sedge warblers, but the meadow pipits came instead, and the whitethroats only moved farther on.

Because I burnt all the old heather for the sake of the sea pies, the wheatears and the sheep, the stonechats nested away on the mainland, but they were good enough to bring back a fledged brood to feed in the garden.

The choughs hung about so late that I felt sure of a nest by June, yet they vanished, and in their place a pair of shags nested in the same ravine in Mad Bay. Then a white owl disappeared too, leaving the island to a silent, evil little owl, whose four eggs were laid upon ninety-eight quill feathers of the storm petrel (its favourite food here), in a hole under a slab of rock facing the wild tides at the Head.

The ravens reared four, but all through the year the buzzards did naught but line their nest with flowers, and sit about ornamentally, if sluggishly, on the higher rocks. I think the female, a huge hoary bird, has grown too old to lay eggs. They lived exclusively on rabbits until the shearwater exodus began.

All other birds behaved normally save those of the shearwater colony behind the house, which seemed to be seized with a fever to enlarge and extend their burrows on every dark night in the past summer. They excavated so vigorously that they broke into each other's burrows; their eggs rolled together and they quarrelled over and incubated their neighbours' eggs until absolute confusion reigned. I did my best to restore order, and many times replaced eggs thrown out in the scuffles, but the dead-in-shell mortality was heavy. After twenty-four hours in a freezing wind outside the burrow a partially hatched chick was still alive in the shell, and ultimately emerged when returned to the breast of its parent. This egg had already suffered so many vagaries that it hatched thirteen days overdue, making an incubation period of sixty-three days!

Year after year the same pairs of shearwaters return to this colony. The numbered leg rings they wear grow thinner each year through contact with salt air and water, and are soon defaced. To be on the safe side we now substitute new rings each year. The same pairs keep fairly regularly to the same burrows. AE 688 (or Caroline), our most precious bird, must now be at least eleven years old.

Experiments with puffins, as well as with other sea birds are being carried out on the same lines, and meanwhile we have worked out part of the life history of the young puffin in its first year. Nothing was known of how the young puffin reached the sea. We can now dispel the belief that the parents carry it down. On the contrary, the old puffins, like the shearwaters, suddenly desert the portly fledgeling, having overfed him so long, and go off to sea to moult their faded and worn plumage. The young one lives for several days, camel-like, off its own fat. Its high cheeping hunger call, unanswered, gradually ceases. It remains fasting and sitting near the mouth of the burrow, too timid to venture abroad. But at last, after four or five days, the forces it has so long resisted drive it forth from the burrow and into the sea.

Despite the fact that when adult the species is entirely diurnal on land, the young one (and this must be noted as a sign of inherited wisdom) walks to the sea only by night. Nothing is more enchanting than to go out of doors on July and August nights and wander along the cliffs in search of young puffins on the march. Lacking the brilliance of the parents, dark-beaked and -footed, they have a sober, dignified air as they leisurely, uprightly, goosestep in the glare of our torch. Coming to a downward slope they will suddenly take wing, not always reaching the sea at the first attempt. We find them in the mornings imprisoned in the garden or in the folds, bewildered after a series of bad take-offs. We take them to the sea, and mark how, on touching the water, they dive and dive, often and long. Only in this manner, by leading a life half submarine at sea, and wholly nocturnal on land, until it can learn to fly strongly, does the young puffin defeat the gulls, which would otherwise exterminate it.

This desertion by the parents explained one thing which had puzzled me on the day in August six years ago that I made my second crossing to the island. It explained why I saw the fledgeling puffins swimming apart from the groups of adults, never following their parents, as were the young razorbills and guillemots.

TWENTY-FIVE

Happily ever after

EARLY SPRING AND SUMMER is the sweetest time of the island year, when each day brings more sunshine, birds and flowers. Life then is one long round of busy pleasure.

Shepherding is full of interest and expectation at this time. I walk each day around the island, counting the flock and tending the ewes with lambs; making sure that they have sought shelter on windy days, and that all is well. I confess it is an easy task, and much to my liking, this long perambulation along the cliffs, counting my precious flock, and welcoming the newborn lambs and seeing that they are able to stand sturdily on their long legs and take nourishment.

The sheep are quite wise to the weather, and save me much trouble by always retiring to the lee side of the island in bad weather. Here, behind rock outcrops and on the cliff slopes they have perfect shelter from the wind. They graze happily on the coarse grass, campion and thrift. Because we keep only one quiet old dog the sheep are very tame, as are our goats; and we have little trouble in examining them at any time. The flock, which varies each year, numbers about fifty, headed by his majesty Crag, the black-faced ram. They are mostly cross-bred, with a strain of the hardy Welsh mountain breed, which is well suited to grazing on rough, exposed land.

In walking every day around the island upon this work I am able to satisfy my desire to know how my little kingdom progresses, what new arrivals are here, what birds gone: whether the tadpoles are hatched under the starwort in the main pond, whether the lesser black-backs have yet occupied the bog, whether the ravens have brought their young off, whether any black redstarts have come, whether the vernal squills, the campion or the cowslips are flowering, and a hundred other events of early spring. In summer the thousand daily events and adventures of the walk are almost bewildering. On hot days, when the long walk over rough ground and through bracken and heather – perhaps for four miles – following the indentations of the coastline, is likely to exhaust too much energy and time, the pony is saddled, and the rounding-up is accomplished at a gallop.

Time is precious in summer. Early in the morning we drive in the flock to the folds before breakfast, and while the grass is yet wet with dew. First one of us gallops off to the end of the island on Punch, and drives in the outlying ewes and half-grown lambs, while the other, on foot, brings in the nearer sheep. Punch is of a mountain breed, like the sheep, and knows how to gallop over rough ground and how to recover his balance – if he steps into a rabbit hole – without throwing his rider. Once in the main fold the flock is examined with the eye for signs of fly attacks, counted, and then released. In June comes shearing time, and from July onwards the unwanted lambs and ewes are sold off to dealers on the mainland.

When we have examined the sheep, and have had breakfast, the main work of the day begins. We hurry off to the day's fishing, eager to see what wondrous things of the sea we have caught in our basket pots, and all day long we are in the boat at this pleasant task. The pots are usually baited each with three pieces of gurnet for the snaring of lobsters, crayfish and crabs, and, although we get our fair share of these, we also have many unexpected hauls of such fish as conger eels, cuttlefish, jellyfish, starfish, sea slugs, prawns, 'spider' and other crabs, and many another strange-looking creature of the deep.

The pots, which we ourselves make out of withies, in the slack period at the end of winter, are tied on a long line, twelve to each 'string.' The ends of the string are then buoyed with corks, to mark the spot where the string is 'shot' into the water. The pots themselves are each weighted with two stones to make them sink to the bed of the sea. In some years we have worked as many as six of these strings, a total of seventy-two pots, shot at various points around the island coast, hauling all of them as often as four times each day in favourable weather. But usually, thirty pots are as much as we can, with other duties, comfortably manage. Sometimes we try our luck farther afield and shoot a string of pots at Grassholm. Once a week the accumulated catch of shellfish is taken to the mainland and marketed.

From our goats we obtain milk, butter and cheese; from our garden, fruit and the produce of the soil; from the chickens and gulls, eggs; from the island and the sea, rabbits and fish. We have only to grow and grind our own wheat in order to be self-supporting. I have even suggested to Doris that we spin our own wool and weave our own garments! So far, however, we rely on others for these items, and I think we are well entitled to do so, so long as our exports of sheep, wool, rabbits and fish pay for these imports.

From the sea we obtain our firewood. So far the coal from the schooner has lasted us well, together with the peat dug from the 'turbary' on the bog. This 'turbary,' an area of a few acres, supplied the fuel of turf or peat which the inhabitants of the island used over a hundred years ago.

The talk of peat brings me thus late to the history of the island, of which very little appears to be known. Fenton, in his *Tour Through Pembrokeshire*, of 1811, describes the house as having been built in a 'whimsical manner, with suitable farm offices' by a gentleman. He offers no date of building, but from what little evidence I can gather it must have been constructed not later than 1750, and probably earlier by some decades. The inhabitants of the farm in those days, when they stood in need of anything, lit a fire on a high rock as a signal for a boat to attend them. If they required flour for bread they lit the fire on a high rock in the centre of the island; this rock being known even now as Bread Rock; if urgent medical assistance was needed the fire was lit on the top of Spy Rock, the easternmost prominence as viewed from the mainland.

Those were days when telegraphy was almost unknown. Now, if we should ever be in dire need of medical aid, or other assistance, and it were impossible to use our boat at the time, we should have recourse to signalling the coastguards at St Ann's Head by means of a morse lantern, and could, if necessary, send a telegram at any time by such means.

Happily, illnesses are infrequent in this healthy, salt air. The coast-dwelling folk of Pembrokeshire have a reputation for longevity, and I like to picture myself an old salt, with a flowing white beard, and at eighty years of age still hauling my pots and driving my sheep. But Doris, as yet, does not approve of a beard.

Thus you will see that my one-time dreams have come true, for my wife and I dwell on an island, far from the turmoil of a city, and accessible only to the chosen few. If we have few of the modern amenities of civilisation, we have in full measure the glory of the sea and the winds and the sky. We have a rich show of sea-loving flowers. We have seals and sheep and goats. We have all the birds we could wish for, and welcome everyone; in the summer there are over thirty thousand on our island, of which two thirds comprise puffins and shearwaters. In variety, so far, well over a hundred different species are recorded, and there is a peculiar delight in welcoming new species in such a well-defined area as an island.

Each summer brings us fresh cruising adventures, and when the north wind is true and steady we shall be sailing once more out to distant Grassholm, to see again the gannets and seals.

And so live happily ever after!

The entrance to 'Nest A' in the knoll colony

List of birds recorded at Skokholm 1927–1940
(B. = breeding or has bred)

Raven (*Corvus c. corax* L.). B.
Hooded crow (*Corvus c. comix* L.).
Carrion-crow (*Corvus c. corone* L.). B.
Rook (*Corvus f. frugilegus* L.).
Jackdaw (*Corvus monedula spermologus* Vieill.).
Chough (*Pyrrhocorax p. pyrrhocorax* L.). B.
Starling (*Sturnus v. vulgaris* L.). B.
Greenfinch (*Chloris ch. chloris* L.).
British goldfinch (*Carduelis c. britannica* Hart.).
Twite (*Carduelis flavirostris pipilans* Latham).
Linnet (*Carduelis c. cannabina* L.). B.
Crossbill (*Loxia c. curvirostra* L.).
Chaffinch (*Fringilla coelebs gengleri* Kleinschmidt).
Brambling (*Fringilla montifringilla* L.).
Corn bunting (*Emberiza calandra* L.).
Yellow bunting (*Emberiza c. citrinella* L.).
Ortolan bunting (*Emberiza hortulana* L.).
Reed bunting (*Emberiza s. schoeniclus* L.).
Lapland bunting (*Calcarius l. lapponicus* L.).
Snow bunting (*Plectrophenax n. nivalis* L.).
House sparrow (*Passer d. domesticus* L.).
Tree sparrow (*Passer m. montanus* L.).
Skylark (*Alauda a. arvensis* L.). B.
Tree pipit (*Anthus t. trivialis* L.).
Meadow pipit (*Anthus pratensis* L.). B.
Water pipit (*Anthus s. spinoletta* L.).
Rock pipit (*Anthus spinoletta petrosus* Mont.). B.
Yellow wagtail (*Motacilla flava flavissima* Blyth).
Grey wagtail (*Motacilla c. cinerea* Tunst.).
Pied wagtail (*Motacilla alba yarrellii* Gould). B.
White wagtail (*Motacilla a. alba* L.).
British tree-creeper (*Certhia familiaris britannica* Ridgw.).

Coal tit (*Parus ater britannicus* Sharpe and Dress.).
Red-backed shrike (*Lanius c. collurio* L.).
Spotted flycatcher (*Muscicapa s. striata* Pall.).
Pied flycatcher (*Muscicapa h. hypoleuca* Pall.).
Goldcrest (*Regulus regulus anglorum* Hart.).
Chiffchaff (*Phylloscopus c. collybita* Vieill.).
Willow warbler (*Phylloscopus t. trochilus* L.).
Northern willow warbler (*Phylloscopus trochilus acredula* L.).
Grasshopper warbler (*Locustella n. naevia* Bodd.).
Sedge warbler (*Acrocephalus schoenobaenus* L.). B.
Garden warbler (*Sylvia borin* Bodd.).
Blackcap (*Sylvia a. atricapilla* L.).
Whitethroat (*Sylvia c. communis* Latham). B.
Lesser whitethroat (*Sylvia c. curruca* L.).
Fieldfare (*Turdus pilaris* L.).
Mistle thrush (*Turdus v. viscivorus* L.).
British song thrush (*Turdus e. ericetorum* Turton).
Continental song thrush (*Turdus ericetorum philomelus* Brehm).
Redwing (*Turdus m. musicus* L.).
Ring ouzel (*Turdus t. torquatus* L.).
Blackbird (*Turdus m. merula* L.). B.
Wheatear (*Oenanthe ce. amanthe* L.). B.
Greenland wheatear (*Oenanthe oenanthe leucorrhoa* Gm.).
Whinchat (*Saxicola rubetra* L.).
Stonechat (*Saxicola torquata hibernans* Hart.). B.
Redstart (*Phoenicurus ph. phoenicurus* L.).
Black redstart (*Phoenicurus ochrurus gibraltariensis* Gm.).
Robin (*Erithacus rubecula melophilus* Hart.). B.
Hedge sparrow (*Prunella modularis occidentalis* Hart.). B.
Wren (*Troglodytes t. troglodytes* L.).
Swallow (*Hirundo r. rustica* L.). B.
House martin (*Delichon u. urbica* L.).
Sand martin (*Riparia r. riparia* L.).
Swift (*Apus a. apus* L.).
Nightjar (*Caprimulgus e. europaeus* L.).
Hoopoe (*Upupa e. epops* L.).
Kingfisher (*Alcedo atthis ispida* L.).
Wryneck (*Jynx t. torquilla* L.).
Cuckoo (*Cuculus c. canorus* L.). B.
Little owl (*Athene noctua vidalii* A. E. Brehm). B.

Short-eared owl (*Asio f. flammeus* Pontopp.).
Barn owl (*Tyto a. alba* Scop.).
Peregrine falcon (*Falco p. peregrinus* Tunst.). B.
Merlin (*Falco columbarius cesalon* Tunst.).
Kestrel (*Falco t. tinnunculus* L.).
Buzzard (*Buteo b. buteo* L.). B.
Montagu's harrier (*Circus pygargus* L.).
Sparrowhawk (*Accipiter n. nisus* L.).
Common heron (*Ardea c. cinerea* L.).
White-fronted goose (*Anser a. albifrons* L.).
Shelduck (*Tadorna tadorna* L.).
Mallard (*Anas p. platyrhyncha* L.). B.
Teal (*Anas c. crecca* L.).
Wigeon (*Anas penelope* L.).
Shoveler (*Spatula clypeata* L.).
Common scoter (*Melanitta n. nigra* L.).
Cormorant (*Phalacrocorax c. carbo* L.).
Shag (*Phalacrocorax a. aristotelis* L.). B.
Gannet (*Sula bassana* L.).
Storm petrel (*Hydrobates pelagicus* L.). B.
Manx shearwater (*Puffinus p. puffinus* Brunn.). B.
Sooty shearwater (*Puffinus griseus* Gm.).
Fulmar petrel (*Fulmarus g. glacialis* L.).
Little grebe (*Podiceps r. ruficollis* Pall.).
Great northern diver (*Colymbus immer* Brunn.).
Black-throated diver (*Colymbus a. arcticus* L.).
Red-throated diver (*Colymbus stellatus* Pontopp.).
Wood pigeon (*Columba p. palumbus* L.).
Stock dove (*Columba cenas* L.).
Turtle dove (*Streptopelia t. turtur* L.).
Bar-tailed godwit (*Limosa I. lapponica* L.).
Black-tailed godwit (*Limosa I. limosa* L.).
Common curlew (*Numenius a. arquata* L.).
Whimbrel (*Numenius ph. phoeopus* L.).
Woodcock (*Scolopax rusticola* L.).
Common snipe (*Capella g. gallinago* L.).
Jack snipe (*Lymnocryptes minimus* Brunn.).
Turnstone (*Arenaria i. interpres* L.).
Knot (*Calidris c. canutus* L.).

Southern dunlin (*Calidris alpina schinzii* Brehm).
Little stint (*Calidris minuta* Leisl.).
Common sandpiper (*Actitis hypoleucos* L.).
Purple sandpiper (*Calidris m. maritima* Brunn.).
Sanderling (*Crocethia alba* Pall.).
Ruff (*Philomachus pugnax* L.).
Redshank (*Tringa totanus britannica* Math.).
Greenshank (*Tringa nebularia* Gunn.).
Ringed plover (*Charadrius h. hiaticula* L.).
Golden plover (*Pluvialis a. apricaria* L.).
Grey plover (*Squatarola squatarola* L.).
Lapwing (*Vanellus vanellus* L.). B.
British oystercatcher (*Hoematopus ostralegus occidentalis* Neum.).
Stone curlew (*Burhinus ce. oedicnemus* L.).
Sandwich tern (*Sterna s. sandvicensis* Lath.).
Roseate tern (*Sterna d. dougallii* Mont.).
Common tern (*Sterna h. hirundo* L.).
Arctic tern (*Sterna macrura* Naumann).
Little tern (*Sterna a. albifrons* Pall.).
Black-headed gull (*Larus r. ridibundus* L.).
Common gull (*Larus c. canus* L.).
Herring gull (*Larus a. argentatus* Pont.). B.
Scandinavian lesser black-backed gull (*Larus f. fuscus* L.).
British lesser black-backed gull (*Larus fuscus graellsii* Brehm). B.
Great black-backed gull (*Larus marinus* L.). B.
Kittiwake (*Rissa t. tridactyla* L.).
Arctic skua (*Stercorarius parasiticus* L.).
British razorbill (*Alca torda britannica* Ticehurst). B.
Northern guillemot (*Uria a. aalge* Pont.).
Southern guillemot (*Uria aalge albionis* With.). B.
Black guillemot (*Uria g. grylle* L.).
Little auk (*Alle a. alle* L.).
Southern puffin (*Fratercula arctica grabae* Brehm). B.
Corncrake (*Crex crex* L.). B.
Water-rail (*Rallus a. aquaticus* L.). B.
Moorhen (*Gallinula ch. chloropus* L.). B.
Coot (*Fulica a. atra* L.).
Quail (*Coturnix c. coturnix* L.).

List of flora recorded at Skokholm 1927–1940

Water crowfoot (*Ranunculus aquatilis* L. agg.).
Lesser spearwort (*Ranunculus flammula* L.).
Lesser celandine (*Ranunculus ficaria* L.).
Creeping buttercup (*Ranunculus repens* L.).
Ivy-leaved crowfoot (*Ranunculus hederaceus* L.).
Field poppy (*Papaver rhozas* L.).
G. Common watercress (*Nasturtium officinale* Br. agg.).
Lady's smock (*Cardamine pratensis* L.).
Hairy bittercress (*Cardamine hirsuta* L.).
Charlock (*Brassica arvense* Kuntze.).
Scurvy grass (*Cochlearia officinalis* L.).
Danish scurvy grass (*Cochlearia danica* L.).
English scurvy grass (*Cochlearia anglica* L.).
Shepherd's-purse (*Capsella bursa-pastoris* Medik.).
Lesser swine-cress (*Coronopus didymus* L., Sm.).
Dog violet (*Viola riviniana* Reichb.).
Heartsease (*Viola tricolor* L. agg.).
Sea-pansy (*Viola curtisii* Forst.).
Milkwort (*Polygala vulgare* L.).
Sea campion (*Silene maritima* With.).
Red campion (*Lychnis dioica* L.).
Sea pearlwort (*Sagina maritima* Don).
Thyme-leaved sandwort (*Arenaria serpyllifolia* L.).
Mouse-ear chickweed (*Cerostium cerastium* L.).
　　　　　　　　　　(*Cerastium tetrandum* Curt.).
　　　　　　　　　　(*Cerastium vulgatum* L.).
Chickweed (*Stellaria media* Vill.).
Bog stitchwort (*Stellaria alsine* Grimm).
Lesser stitchwort (*Stellaria graminea* L.).
Sand spurrey (*Spergularia rupicola* Lebel).
Corn spurrey (*Spergula arvensis* L. agg.).
G. Water blinks (*Montia fontana* L.).

Trailing St John's wort (*Hypericum humifusum* L.).
Marsh St John's wort (*Hypericum elodes* L.).
Allseed (*Radiola linoides* Roth).
Tree mallow (*Lavatera arborea* L.).
Sea stork's-bill (*Erodium maritimum* L'Hérit.).
Sycamore (*Acer pseudo-platanus* L.).
Furze (*Ulex europaeus* L.).
Red clover (*Trifolium pratense* L.).
White clover (*Trifolium repens* L.).
Lesser clover (*Trifolium dubium* Sibth.).
Bird's-foot trefoil (*Lotus corniculatus* L.).
Kidney vetch (*Anthyllis vulneraria* L.).
Common vetch (*Vicia sativa* L.).
Blackthorn (*Prunus spinosa* L.).
Meadow sweet (*Spiraea ulmaria* L.).
Bramble (*Rubus fruticosus* L. agg.).
Tormentil (*Potentilla erecta* L., Hampe).
Silverweed (*Potentilla anserina* L.).
Spring potentilla (*Potentilla verna* L.).
Marsh willowherb (*Epilobium palustre* L.).
Water purslane (*Peplis portula* L.).
Pennywort (*Cotyledon umbilicus* L.).
English stonecrop (*Sedum anglicum* Huds.).
Marsh pennywort (*Hydrocotyle vulgaris* L.).
Lesser marshwort (*Apium inundatum* (L.) H.G. Reichb.).
Marshwort (*Apium nodiflorum* (L.) H.G. Reichb.).
Hemlock water-dropwort (*Oenanthe crocata* L.).
Samphire (*Crithmum maritimum* L.).
Cow parsnip (*Heracleum sphondylium* L.).
Sea carrot (*Daucus gummifer* L.).
Hemlock (*Conium maculatum* L.).
Ivy (*Hedera helix* L.).
Common elder (*Sambucus nigra* L.).
Common honeysuckle (*Lonicera periclymenum* L.)
Heath bedstraw (*Galium saxatile* L.).
Lady's bedstraw (*Galium verum* L.).
Marsh bedstraw (*Galium palustre* L.).
Woodruff (*Asperula odorata* L.).
Hemp agrimony (*Eupatorium cannabinum* L.)

Golden rod (*Solidago virgaurea* L.).
Daisy (*Bellis perennis* L.).
Ox-eye daisy (*Chrysanthemum leucanthemum* L.).
Corn marigold (*Chrysanthemum segetum* L.).
Sea mayweed (*Matricaria maritima* L.).
Yarrow (*Achillea millefolium* L.).
Groundsel (*Senecio vulgaris* L.).
Sticky groundsel (*Senecio viscosus* L.).
Ragwort (*Senecio jacobaea* L.).
Wood groundsel (*Senecio sylvaticus* L.).
Burdock (*Arctium lappa* L.).
Spear thistle (*Cirsium vulgare* (Savi) Airy-Shaw).
Marsh thistle (C. *palustre* Scop.).
Creeping thistle (C. *arvense* Scop.).
Knapweed (*Centaurea nigra* L. agg.).
Great knapweed (*Centaurea scabiosa* L.).
Autumnal hawkbit (*Leontodon autumnalis* L.).
Cat's ear (*Hypochceris radicata* L.).
Corn sowthistle (*Sonchus arvensis* L.).
Dandelion (*Taraxacum officinale* Weber).
Sheep's bit (*Jasione montana* L.).
Bell heather (*Erica cinerea* L.).
Ling (*Calluna vulgaris* (L.) Hull).
Primrose (*Primula vulgaris* Huds.).
Cowslip (*Primula veris* L.).
Pimpernel (*Anagallis arvensis* L.).
Bog pimpernel (*Anagallis tenella* L., Murr.).
Brookweed (*Samolus valerandi* L.).
Ash (*Fraxinus excelsior* L.). G.
Privet (*Ligustrum vulgare* L.).
Centaury (*Centaurium umbellatum* Gilib.).
Water forget-me-not (*Myosotis scorpioides* L. em., Hill).
Field forget-me-not (*Myosotis arvensis* L. Hill).
Early forget-me-not (*Myosotis collina* Hoffm.).
Yellow and blue forget-me-not (*Myosotis versicolor* Sm.).
Borage (*Borago officinalis* L.).
Bittersweet (*Solanum dulcamara* L.).
Figwort (*Scrophularia nodosa* L.).
Foxglove (*Digitalis purpurea* L.).

Germander speedwell (*Veronica chamaedrys* L.).
Common speedwell (*Veronica officinalis* L.).
Procumbent speedwell (*Veronica agrestis* L.).
Wall speedwell (*Veronica arvensis* L.).
Eyebright (*Euphrasia officinalis* L. agg.).
Red rattle (*Pedicularis palustris* L.).
Lousewort (*Pedicularis sylvatica* L.).
Water mint (*Mentha aquatica* L.).
Wild thyme (*Thymus serpyllum* L.).
Ground Ivy (*Nepeta hederacea* L., Trev.).
Self heal (*Prunella vulgaris* L.).
Lesser skullcap (*Scutellaria minor* Huds.).
Field woundwort (*Stachys arvensis* L.).
Common hemp-nettle (*Galeopsis tetrahit* L.).
Henbit (*Lamium amplexicaule* L.).
Red dead-nettle (*Lamium purpureum* L.).
Wood sage (*Teucrium scorodonia* L.).
Common bugle (*Ajuga reptans* L.).
Thrift, sea pink (*Statice maritima* Mill.).
Ribwort (*Plantago lanceolata* L.).
Sea plantain (*Plantago maritima* L.).
Bucks-horn plantain (*Plantago coronopus* L.).
Greater plantain (*Plantago major* L.).
Shoreweed (*Littorella uniflora* L., Aschers.).
Red goosefoot (*Chenopodium rubrum* L.).
White goosefoot (*Chenopodium album* L.).
Wild beet (*Beta maritima* L.).
Orache (*Atriplex hastata* L.).
Sea orache (*Atriplex glabriuscula* Edmonst.).
Curled dock (*Rumex crispus* L.).
Sorrel (*Rumex acetosa* L.).
Sheep's sorrel (*Rumex acetosella* L.).
Knotgrass (*Polygonum aviculare* L.).
Amphibious polygonum (*Polygonum amphibium* L.).
Spotted persicaria (*Polygonum persicaria* L.).
Waterpepper (*Polygonum hydropiper* L.).
Sun spurge (*Euphorbia helioscopia* L.).
Petty spurge (*Euphorbia peplus* L.).
Dwarf spurge (*Euphorbia exigua* L.).
Water starwort (*Callitriche aquatica* agg.).

Small nettle (*Urtica urens* L.).
Common nettle (*Urtica dioica* L.).
Creeping willow (*Salix repens* L.).
Cuckoo-pint (*Arum maculatum* L.).
Lesser duckweed (*Lemna minor* L.).
Floating pondweed (*Potamogeton natans* L.).
Lesser water plantain (*Alisma ranunculoides* L.).
Early purple orchid (*Orchis mascula* L.).
Marsh orchid (*Orchis incarnata* L.).
Daffodil (*Narcissus pseudo-narcissus* L.). Planted.
Snowdrop (*Galanthus nivalis* L.). Planted.
Spring squill (*Scilla verna* Huds.).
Bluebell (*Scilla non-scripta* (L.) H. and L.).
Toad rush (*Juncus bufonius* L.).
Common rush (*Juncus communis* agg.).
Heath rush (*Juncus squarrosus* L.).
Field woodrush (*Luzula campestris* L. DC).
Tufted sedge (*Carex goodenowii* Gay).
Vernal sedge (*Carex caryophyllea* Latour).
Downy oatgrass (*Avena pubescens* Huds.).
Yorkshire fog (*Holcus lanatus* L.).
Couch grass (*Agropyrum repens* L.).
Cock's-foot grass (*Dactylis glomerata* L.).
Crested dog's-tail grass (*Cynosurus cristatus* L.).
Annual meadow grass (*Poa annua* L.).
Smooth meadow grass (*Poa pratensis* L.).
Rough meadow grass (*Poa trivialis* L.).
Silvery hair-grass (*Aira caryophyllea* L.).
Sheep's fescue (*Festuca ovina* L.).
Common reed (*Phragmites vulgaris* Lam. Crép.).
Male fern (*Dryopteris filix-mas* (L. Schott.)
Sea spleenwort (*Asplenium marinum* L.).
Hart's-tongue fern (*Phyllitis scolopendrium* (L. Newm.).
Hard fern (*Blechnum spicant* L. With.).
Bracken (*Pteridium aquilinum* L. Kuhn).

Please contact Little Toller Books
to join our mailing list or for more information
on current and forthcoming titles.

Nature Classics Library

IN THE COUNTRY *Kenneth Allsop*
THE JOURNAL OF A DISAPPOINTED MAN *W.N.P. Barbellion*
DOWN THE RIVER *H.E. Bates*
THROUGH THE WOODS *H.E. Bates*
APPLE ACRE *Adrian Bell*
MEN AND THE FIELDS *Adrian Bell*
THE MILITARY ORCHID *Jocelyn Brooke*
THE MIRROR OF THE SEA *Joseph Conrad*
ISLAND YEARS, ISLAND FARM *Frank Fraser Darling*
THE PATTERN UNDER THE PLOUGH *George Ewart Evans*
A TIME FROM THE WORLD *Rowena Farre*
SWEET THAMES RUN SOFTLY *Robert Gibbings*
THE MAKING OF THE ENGLISH LANDSCAPE *W.G. Hoskins*
A SHEPHERD'S LIFE *W.H. Hudson*
WILD LIFE IN A SOUTHERN COUNTY *Richard Jefferies*
BROTHER TO THE OX *Fred Kitchen*
FOUR HEDGES *Clare Leighton*
DREAM ISLAND *R.M. Lockley*
LETTERS FROM SKOKHOLM *R.M. Lockley*
HOME COUNTRY *Richard Mabey*
THE UNOFFICIAL COUNTRYSIDE *Richard Mabey*
RING OF BRIGHT WATER *Gavin Maxwell*
FRESH WOODS, PASTURES NEW *Ian Niall*
EARTH MEMORIES *Llewelyn Powys*
IN PURSUIT OF SPRING *Edward Thomas*
THE SOUTH COUNTRY *Edward Thomas*
THE NATURAL HISTORY OF SELBORNE *Gilbert White*
THE SHINING LEVELS *John Wyatt*

LITTLE TOLLER BOOKS
Lower Dairy Toller Fratrum Dorset DT2 OEL

Telephone: 01300 321536
books@littletoller.co.uk
www.littletoller.co.uk